THE NEW MERMAIDS

Volpone

THE NEW MERMAIDS

General Editors

PHILIP BROCKBANK

Professor of English, York University

BRIAN MORRIS

Senior Lecturer in English, York University

Volpone

BEN JONSON

Edited by PHILIP BROCKBANK

ERNEST BENN LIMITED
LONDON

First published in this form 1968
by Ernest Benn Limited
Bouverie House · Fleet Street · London · EC4
© *Ernest Benn Limited 1968*
Distributed in Canada by
The General Publishing Company Limited · Toronto
Printed in Great Britain

510-33661-2

Paperback 510-33666-3

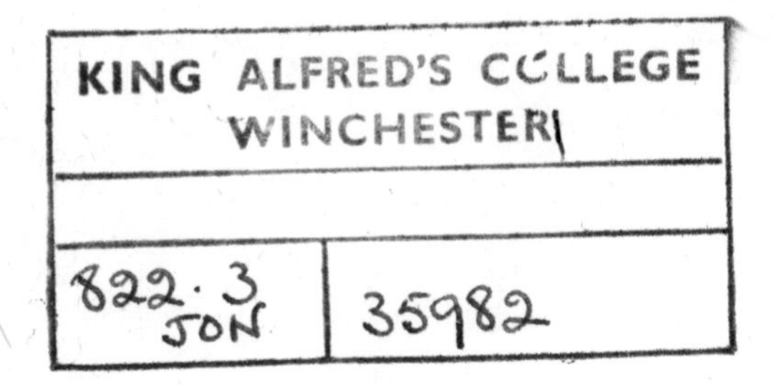
KING ALFRED'S COLLEGE
WINCHESTER
822.3
JON
35982

CONTENTS

Illustrations vi
Introduction vii
The Author vii
The Play ix
The Play on the Stage xxvii
The Text and its Presentation xxxi
A Note on the Notes xxxvii
Acknowledgements xxxviii
Further Reading xxxviii
VOLPONE 1
The Dedication 3
The Epistle 5
The Persons of the Play 11
The Argument 13
The Prologue 13
The Text 14
Appendix I: Analogues and Documents 157
Legacy Hunting 157
The Afflictions of Age 159
The Venetian Scene 161
Possession and Imposture 165
Appendix II: A Selection of Variants 167

ILLUSTRATIONS

Figure 1 'Hood an ass with reverend purple,
So you can hide his two ambitious ears,
And, he shall pass for a cathedral doctor.'

The illustration is from Holbein's engravings to Erasmus's *Praise of Folly*, see page 23.

Figure 2 Stage structure simplified from an arcade of honour, Brussels, 1594. The figures in the original illustration have been omitted.

Figure 3 A Mountebank Stage, *c.* 1600.

Figures 2 and 3 appear in C. Walter Hodges, *The Globe Restored* (London, 1953).

INTRODUCTION

THE AUTHOR

BEN JONSON was born a Londoner in 1572, the posthumous son of an impoverished gentleman. His mother married a bricklayer shortly afterwards, and his circumstances in youth were decidedly straitened. Through the intervention of an outsider, however, he had some education at Westminster School under William Camden, who remained a lifelong friend; but he probably did not finish school and certainly did not go on, as most of his contemporaries there did, to Oxford or Cambridge. Instead he was apprenticed, probably in his stepfather's craft, about 1589, remaining in it long enough only to learn he 'could not endure' it. Before 1597 he had volunteered to serve in Flanders where, during a lull in the fighting, 'in the face of both the camps', he met and killed one of the enemy in single combat and returned from no-man's-land with his victim's weapons. The scene is an emblem for his life: the giant figure, a party to neither faction, warring alone in the classical manner before his awed onlookers.

Sometime in the early 1590s he married. By the time he was twenty-five he was playing the lead in Kyd's *Spanish Tragedy* for the theatrical manager and entrepreneur Philip Henslowe. As a writer he may also have composed additions to Kyd's work; he certainly did so for Nashe's satirical *Isle of Dogs*, and was imprisoned for the 'slandrous matter' in it. But already by 1598 Francis Meres listed him in *Palladis Tamia* amongst 'our best for tragedy' along with Kyd himself and Shakespeare. These tragedies, and indeed all the work of his early twenties, have vanished, but in the surviving records the man bursts upon the theatrical scene with characteristic and transforming energy.

In 1598 as well his first great success in comedy, *Every Man in his Humour*, was produced; in this, as in *Sejanus*, Shakespeare played a leading role. Within the same month Jonson killed an actor in Henslowe's company, Gabriel Spencer, in a duel. He pleaded guilty to a charge of felony and saved himself from the gallows only by claiming 'benefit of clergy', that is, by proving his literacy and hence immunity by reading 'neck-verse'. His goods—such as they may have been—were confiscated and he was branded on the thumb. His career was not yet fully under way: in writing of the incident, Henslowe refers to Jonson as a 'bricklayer'.

Still in the same year *The Case is Altered* was acted, once again with great success, and in 1599 or 1600 came *Every Man Out of his Humour*, which—although it too enhanced his growing reputation—included in the targets of its satire the diction of some contemporary playwrights, notably John Marston. Marston may have annoyed his older friend by a bungled attempt to flatter him in *Histriomastix* a few months earlier, but he was in any case ready to take very unfriendly revenge for *Every Man Out* when, in late 1600, he caricatured Jonson in *Jack Drum's Entertainment*. Jonson countered with *Cynthia's Revels*, Marston with *What You Will*, Jonson with *Poetaster*, all in 1601. Thomas Dekker, previously Jonson's collaborator on the lost tragedy *Page of Plymouth*, came to Marston's aid with *Satiro-mastix*. But Jonson had gone beyond attacking his attackers: his plays, and particularly *Poetaster*, satirised influential men, and he barely escaped prosecution again. He withdrew, not yet thirty years old, from comedy and the popular stage, into the patronage and protection first of Sir Robert Townshend and later of Esmé Stewart, Lord Aubigny, to whom he dedicated the fruit of his retirement, *Sejanus*.

Once again Jonson's talent for trouble caused him difficulty with the authorities, this time on the pretext of 'popery and treason'—he had become a Catholic during his imprisonment for killing Spencer—and once again powerful friends intervened to save him. Still again in 1604, when he collaborated with his reconciled friend Marston and with George Chapman on the comedy *Eastward Ho!* he was jailed, now for satirising the Scots, for James I was king. But once more he was let off, and on the whole the accession of James I was of great benefit to Jonson: for this brilliant and learned court he wrote almost all his many masques, delicate confections of erudition and artistry in which he knew no master.

But it is to *Volpone* (1605), *Epicoene* (1609–10), *The Alchemist* (1610), *Bartholomew Fair* (1614) and *The Devil is an Ass* (1616) that we must turn for the central documents of his comic maturity, interrupted only by the tragic (and unsuccessful) *Catiline* of 1611. Jonson had by 1612 become conscious of the scope of his accomplishment, for in that year he began work on a collective edition which would enshrine in an impressive folio the authoritative text. His close connections with the court, doubtless enhanced when he gave up Catholicism about 1610, and the literary self-awareness begot by his huge reading in the classics, in part recorded in his commonplace book *Timber*, led him, unique amongst the playwrights of his age, to take such pains with his *oeuvre*.

Jonson continued writing his masques and non-dramatic poems, but no stage play appeared after *The Devil is an Ass* until *The Staple of News* in 1625. Jonson's fortune declined in the nine years between.

He began them with a walking tour to Scotland in 1618, where Drummond recorded their *Conversations*, and with a visit to Oxford in 1619, where the University made him a Master of Arts. He ended them increasingly destitute of health, money and invention. His rule over the 'tribe' that met at the Mermaid was unweakened, but he depended more and more on pensions from Crown and City, especially when he failed to maintain with Charles I the favour he found with the scholarly James I.

There followed *The New Inn* (1629), *The Magnetic Lady* (1632), and *The Tale of a Tub* (1633); the first was a disaster the last two did little to mitigate. Apart from a few verses he wrote nothing thereafter (his *English Grammar*, a draft of which perished in the fire that destroyed his library in 1623, probably goes back to a period as Professor of Rhetoric at Gresham College), although his lifelong habit of reading was not broken. He did not complete work on the second folio which was to include his writings since 1612. No child of his survived him, and it fell to his intellectual disciples, the 'Sons of Ben', to be his literary executors.

He died on 6 August 1637, at the age of sixty-five, and was buried in Westminster Abbey.

W. F. B.

THE PLAY

Volpone, or *The Fox*, was the work of a single commanding act of the imagination, written in five weeks, making one sustained experience from a great diversity of materials and insights. It carries an air of spontaneity and gay improvisation, and yet it continually wins effects that stand up to exacting reflective analysis. It is an act (to borrow Jonson's rhetoric) 'worthy of celebration', and not a 'declamatory and windy invective'.

The dedicatory Epistle is to the 'Most Equal' (that is, equally just and judicious) Universities of Oxford and Cambridge; the scene is set in Venice; and the first performances were by Shakespeare's company (the King's Men) at the London Globe. These circumstances begin to mark the lineaments of the play; it is a comedy of city-life by a scholar-playwright, and it displays the enterprise and extravagance of Renaissance Venice for the entertainment of a popular English audience. This way of putting it awakens certain expectations and quietens others; the play is about a way of life within a whole society, its implicit judgements and modes of analysis will satisfy the academic mind, and its verve and vitality will engage and delight the public at large.

In the daunting phrases of the Epistle, Jonson may be accounted a 'learned and liberal soul' whose office as comic poet requires him to 'imitate justice', 'instruct to life' and to 'purity of language', and to 'stir up gentle affections'. He will perform for London the services that Horace once performed for Rome; but his responsibilities are equally towards his art—he will 'raise the despised head of poetry again' and 'render her worthy to be embraced, and kissed, of all the great and master spirits of our world'. We may, therefore, survey the play from the platform that Jonson himself has afforded.

THE IMITATION OF JUSTICE

Jonson speaks in his Epistle of the 'strict rigour of *comic* law' and says that his own catastrophe (*dénouement*) may be thought not to accord with it; but the happy ending that would satisfy one kind of pedantry about the nature of comedy, would leave unsatisfied those who clamour for the punishment of vice. Jonson is content to remind his university public that even ancient comedies do not always end happily, but the passage may recall us to the distinct but elusive analogy between comic justice and moral justice—they are not the same but they are often alike. In the final scene Volpone is exposed to the 'strict rigour' not of the comic but of the criminal law; but Jonson insinuates that the judicious will recognise that this is exactly what the comedy itself demands. The comedy requires that comic justice should be executed by the knaves before it is executed upon them.

Jonson is well aware of the contiguity between his own role as plotter of the play's large design, and the roles of the knaves who plot its particular mischiefs. So it happens that the excitements of the play and the nature of its insights owe much to the wit and understanding displayed by Mosca and Volpone as it were on Jonson's behalf. The resourcefulness of the comic playwright, the confidence trickster and the criminal alike, is dramatic and histrionic—they are good at contriving ways out of difficult situations, at putting on an act, and at taking people in. Many of the gloating exchanges between Mosca and Volpone therefore read like Jonson's compliments to his own art—'Good wits are greatest in extremities', 'to make/So rare a music out of discords', 'Scoto himself could hardly have distinguished!'. But the playwright's art is decisively more comprehensive than the knave's, in ways both obvious and subtle.

The gull-and-knave pattern of comic episode has a long history from Aristophanes and Plautus, the Roman *fabulae togatae* (in which the country visitor was often taken in by the city sophisticate) and the *commedia dell'arte*, through Tudor interludes and entertainments and university drama, into the popular comedy of the fifteen-nineties. But it is Jonson (with some prompting from Marlowe's

Jew of Malta) who most fully realises its potentials. The knave of the new plays is not only like the parasite of the old classical plays—exploiting human weakness in order to prosper; he is also like the devil in the medieval moralities—exposing man's weaknesses and feeding their vices to damn them.[1]

Mosca's Justice

Mosca, self-confessedly a parasite and by Volpone called a devil, works to the ends appropriate to both. As a parasite he enjoys the limber wit of the game, its transcendental skill ('dropped from above'); but as a devil he exhibits a perverse mastery of the moral law. When he approaches Bonario under cover of friendship (III.ii) he is like Hypocrisy or Dissimulation in an old play,[2] pretending to be good fellowship in order to serve the devil's ends. His mastery of the appearance and language of virtue moves him to tears and overcomes all the resistance of his allegorically named victim. There is a kind of validity, however, in his claim to 'an interest in the general state/Of goodness, and true virtue' (whether or not Mosca is punning on his different kind of interest in Bonario's estate). All four legacy hunters who attend upon Volpone through Mosca's agency are fittingly abused and tormented for vices that are almost systematically delineated; the seven deadly sins are partners to the gulls' dance but they do not come undisguised—pride, for example, is assimilated into Voltore's forensic vanity, anger finds occasion in Corvino's jealousy and lechery in his lingering upon Aretine (III. vii, 58–64). Envy, gluttony and sloth are subsumed into the pervasive parasitic avarice, the pre-eminent vice of the acquisitive society. Mosca professes this degree of wisdom and upon each gull in turn he passes his derisive sentence:

> Go home, and use the poor Sir Pol, your knight, well;
> For fear I tell some riddles: go, be melancholic. (V.iii, 44–5)

Lady Would-be does indeed (in Jonson's play as well as Mosca's) come 'most melancholic, home'; the same verdict lights upon Corvino, but touched with perverse magnanimity:

> Why, think that these good works
> May help to hide your bad: I'll not betray you . . . (V.iii, 56–7)

[1] For some developments of the devil and the diabolical villain in medieval and Tudor drama, see Bernard Spivack, *Shakespeare and the Allegory of Evil*, 1958.

[2] See, for example, *Lusty Juventus*, *The Disobedient Child*, *Cambyses*, *The Three Lords and Three Ladies of London*, in W. C. Hazlitt (ed.), *Dodsley's Old English Plays*, 15 vol., 1874.

The judgement upon Corbaccio awakens exactly the sensations of physical disgust that Jonson has put to his making:

> Are not you he, that filthy covetous wretch,
> With the three legs, that here, in hope of prey,
> Have, any time this three year, snuffed about,
> With your most grov'ling nose; and would have hired
> Me to the poisoning of my patron? sir?
>
> . . . . Go home, and die, and stink. (V.iii, 67–71, 74)

The displacement of obsequiousness by a purging arrogance (indicated by 'sir?' above) that can be roared out to the deaf ear of Corbaccio in one terrible injunction, is succeeded by the equally effacing, casual and caressing insolence bestowed upon Voltore:

> You, that have so much law, I know ha' the conscience,
> Not to be covetous of what is mine. (V.iii, 97–8)

The gull-and-knave structure as Jonson contrives it allows the knave, therefore, to prevail over the gull not alone because of his superior know-how, but also because of his superior moral insight. He is the scourge of inadequacies and follies, and even of crimes, that the society would have tolerated or overlooked, through inertia or defective government. About *Volpone*, the point can be made the more readily because society itself is directly gulled—both as a public in the Piazza, acclaiming the fake mountebank (himself a charlatan), and as a formal body in the Scrutineo, where the Avocatori are tricked by a knavish display of mock obsequiousness and indulgent moral indignation. The law, as Dogberry cries in *Much Ado About Nothing*, is an ass.

Jonson's Justice

From Bonario's point of view and Celia's, the happy outcome of the action is attributable to divine intervention—'Heaven could not, long, let such gross crimes be hid'. But Jonson knows that divine intervention in a play is the playwright's responsibility ('let no god intervene', says Horace, 'unless a knot come worthy of such a deliverer') and that he must observe, in some sense, the rigour of comic law. It appears that justice is finally imitated (that is, made manifest in the theatre) not by the vigilance of the criminal law, but by the process through which the knaves finally betray each other. It can be known by its commonplace tags and proverbs ('set a thief to catch a thief', 'pride before a fall', 'thieves fall out') but Jonson explores its intellectual and imaginative dynamics, without confining attention to the punishment of vice. Volpone and Mosca are not arbitrarily struck down by their creator's whim or by his servile regard for conventional morality. Jonson's art makes it imperative that they consume themselves with the very energies and fantasies that animate them. To appreciate Jonson's justice we must look more widely at his moral judgements, his poetry and his theatre.

'INSTRUCTION TO LIFE'

Jonson's phrase may be generously interpreted to suggest all the discoveries that the comic-poet makes about the impulses and principles by which men live, both in themselves and in the society about them. Recognising that the play is about virtuosity and is itself a feat of virtuosity, what has virtuosity to do with virtue, and what openings for either did the city cultures of Venice and London provide?

The question in respect to virtuosity has been partly answered—the characteristic vices of the city money-grabbers invited the exercise of the skills of the confidence-trickster. In respect to virtue, it is best considered through the language and postures of the dominant figure, Volpone, fox and magnifico.

Volpone the Magnifico

Usually the conventions of the theatre do not allow us to attribute poetic gifts to the characters of a play (the sentiments are theirs, the arts that convey them are the poet's) but from the profane matins of the opening scene to the closing pun of the last, Volpone is a self-consciously accomplished performer. Jonson's wit plays sardonically upon itself as he touches the parallels between his own talents and his hero's—both inventive, clever mimics, plotters, public entertainers, poets, singers and critics. The mountebank scene seems to be charged with specific allusions to Jonson's own situation,[3] but delight in the rarity of an imposture never wholly disarms judgement.

A good poet, says the Epistle, must be a good man, for it is among the offices of a poet to 'inflame grown men to all great virtues'. But 'virtue' is not an indivisible word describing a definitive group of qualities, and in Jonson's time it was the more complicated because it retained something of its radical Latin sense 'that which becomes a man', together with its current sense 'moral excellence'. There is no necessary tension between manliness and goodness, but their relationship is not a stable one, and the art of the Renaissance often explores and dramatises it; Lady Macbeth's taunt, for instance, and Macbeth's response:

Art thou afeard
To be the same in thine own act and valour
As thou art in desire?

[3] See II.ii, 27 note.

I dare do all that may become a man;
Who dares do more is none.

When you durst do it, then you were a man.
(*Macbeth* I.vii, 39–41, 46–7, 49)

In a different province of moral experience, Volpone's encounter with Celia in the seduction scene is of the same kind. Celia's despair finds expression in a graphic indictment of Venetian morality:

Is that, which ever was a cause of life,
Now placed beneath the basest circumstance?
And modesty an exile made, for money? (III.vii, 136–8)

Volpone, springing from his bed, offers to despise and to transcend the bond that weds her to the impotence of Corvino; he proclaims a higher cause of life than her betrayed and forfeit fidelity:

Ay, in Corvino, and such earth-fed minds,
That never tasted the true heaven of love.
Assure thee, Celia, he that would sell thee,
Only for hope of gain, and that uncertain,
He would have sold his part of paradise
For ready money, had he met a cope-man. (III.vii, 139–44)

Because the contempt for the acquisitive merchant is authentic and just, we are the more ready to entertain the elated assurances of the 'true heaven of love', and to allow the buoyant cadences of the verse to carry speech into song, unresisting. But so to say is manifestly to yield to the seducer. The seducer's persuasive arts have their history in Marlowe, in Catullus, and in the garden of Eden.

Marlowe's early plays tuned English verse to sound those astonishing hubristic hyperboles that make it man's virtue to be a god:

Christian Merchants that with Russian stems
Plough up huge furrows in the Caspian sea,
Shall vail to us, as Lords of all the Lake.

Jove sometime masked in a Shepherd's weed,
And by those steps that he hath scal'd the heavens,
May we become immortal like the Gods.
(*Tamburlaine* I, 387–9, 394–6)

Volpone has a different disdain for merchants:

I use no trade, no venture
.... expose no ships
To threat'nings of the furrow-faced sea. (I.i, 33, 37–8)

and a different aspiration to Olympus:

Whilst we, in changèd shapes, act Ovid's tales,
Thou, like Europa now, and I like Jove,
Then I like Mars, and thou like Erycine,
So, of the rest, till we have quite run through
And wearied all the fables of the gods. (III.vii, 221–5)

But in the movement and range of the imagination there is a significant continuity. Volpone can be represented as indulging the fantasies of a Marlovian hero (for much might be said too of Faustus and Barabas) in a society of corrupt money makers, where the merchants 'expose' their ships to danger but themselves stay home to secure and invest their property—including their wives. Marlowe's Elizabethan eagerness for sovereignty over the plenitude of the earth is still finding expression in Volpone's words to Celia:

See, behold,
What thou art queen of; not in expectation,
As I feed others; but possessed, and crowned. (III.vii, 188–90)

And Volpone has a contempt comparable with Marlowe's for 'earth-bred minds' and for the 'beggar's virtue' (conscience) that he opposes to his own 'wisdom', but where Marlowe's loves of conquest, sensual satisfaction, and knowledge are heroic:

And every warrior that is rapt with love,
Of fame, of valour, and of victory
Must needs have beauty beat on his conceits.
(*Tamburlaine* I, 1961–3)

Volpone's conquests are amorous, his senses look for less aetherial satisfaction, and his knowledge serves for the 'cunning purchase' of his wealth.

While Volpone's vainglory looks back to Marlowe, his lyrical importunity is from Catullus, as Jonson re-creates the celebrated fifth poem (*Vivamus*, *mea Lesbia*, *atque amemus*) to convey yet more poignantly the transcience of the lovers' opportunities. The prospect of an illicit affair in difficult domestic circumstances is transfigured by the song's rhythm and by its easy disdain of ordinary human values:

Why should we defer our joys?
Fame, and rumour are but toys.
Cannot we delude the eyes
Of a few poor household spies? (III.vii, 174–7)

Celia's resistance to Volpone's enticements feels in context like a resistance to the poet's art as well as the seducer's:

Good sir, these things might move a mind affected
With such delights; but I, whose innocence
Is all I can think wealthy, or worth th'enjoying,

And which once lost, I have nought to lose beyond it,
Cannot be taken with these sensual baits. (III.vii, 206–10)

And Jonson is certainly well aware of the strength of the tradition that Volpone represents, with its sense of virtue closely consonant with virility, and sanctioned in pagan mythology by one of Volpone's patron deities, Jove. But the play encompasses both Volpone's virtue and Celia's, and before the scene ends we are made to see the Circean charm give place to gross violence, with 'lust' (the vice in Celia's view most remote from 'manliness') brutally opposed to frigidity and impotence, Volpone's versions of the rival values.

The more conventional kind of goodness embodied in Celia and Bonario is allowed its modicum of strength and resolution, but it is scarcely efficient in the play. It is enough that the master-knaves destroy themselves through over-weening wit and fantasy; like Marlowe's heroes they are over-reachers, whether in self-exhausting, self-consuming phantasmagoria:

> Our drink shall be preparèd gold, and amber;
> Which we will take, until my roof whirl round
> With the vertigo. . . .
>
> And I will meet thee, in as many shapes:
> Where we may, so, transfuse our wand'ring souls,
> Out at our lips, and score up sums of pleasures.
> (III.vii, 217–9, 233–5)

or in self-entangling, self-betraying conspiracy:

> To make a snare, for mine own neck! and run
> My head into it, wilfully! with laughter! (V.xi, 1–2)

Volpone's spell, however, continues to testify to a kind of virtue long after it has been seen for what it is. The bounty that he offers Celia is like that which Mammon in *The Alchemist* would bestow upon the whole of mankind, and it is a travesty of Aristotle's 'magnificence'—the virtue that can only be displayed by a man with great resources (material and spiritual).[4] Nietzsche's Zarathustra supplies the vindicating aphorisms:[5]

> Your soul striveth insatiably for treasures and jewels because your virtue is ever insatiable in the will to give.
>
> Ye compel all things to come unto you and into you, that they may flow back from your fount as gifts of your love.

[4] See Aristotle, *Nicomachean Ethics* IV.ii.

[5] *Thus Spake Zarathustra*, translated by Tille and Bozman, Everyman's Library 1933, pp. 66–7. A comprehensive history of ideas of *Virtù, Virtus* and Virtue could reasonably begin with Zoroaster; but the relevant figures for Jonson are Marlowe and (perhaps) Machiavelli.

But he can also supply the necessary qualification:

> But we hold in horror the degenerate mind that saith:
> 'All for myself!'

Volpone does not, after all, honour and fulfil his role of Magnifico in the Venetian state. The tardy Venetian law does at last discover his weakness and Mosca's:

> These possess wealth, as sick men possess fevers,
> Which, trulier, may be said to possess them. (V.xii, 101–2)

Sir Politic in Venice

The play is so contrived that the episodes of the main plot and the sub-plot seem to belong to the circumambient civilisation. Venice was famed for its mercantile prosperity, its proud resources of gold and treasure, the splendour of its architecture and exuberance of its art, the intensity and ceremony of its public life. Its fame lends resonance to many of the play's local allusions—the Portico to the Procuratia, the Arsenale, and even the Piscaria—and its reputation makes it a probable setting for luxurious living and extravagant fancy; but, as Shakespeare recognises in *The Merchant of Venice*, it is a city of commercial know-how where money can be made by ruthless exploitation.

Thomas Coryat's *Crudities* ('Hastily gobled up in five Moneths travells') is not a source for *Volpone* (it was published in 1611) but, as Herford and Simpson show, it witnesses appropriately to an Englishman's impressions of Venice at the time, and supplies circumstantial glosses on the Venetian scene—from its courtesans to its strappado (see appendix of Analogues and Documents). Coryat, while not always preferring accuracy to human interest, was a good reporter and sufficiently experienced in the ways of the world. It may be that Jonson nevertheless had his eye on Coryat's kind, even (it has been suggested) upon a specific example, another English traveller to Venice, Sir Antony Shirley.[6] However this may be, the presence in the play of Sir Politic and Lady Would-be, and of Peregrine (whose name means both 'hawk' and 'traveller') reminds us of a range of self-deluding fantasies that a foolish Englishman abroad may entertain about foreigners. The Sir Pol episodes are intricately related to the wit of the play without for an instant losing their

[6] The first version of Shirley's book was: *A True Report of Sir Antonie Shirlies Journey overland to Venice, from thence to Seaton, Antioch, Aleppo, and Babilon, and so to Casbine in Persia.* It was published in 1600 but suppressed as unlicensed. A version by William Parry was authorised and published in 1601.

disarming simplicity. Primarily they contribute to the pattern of incidents and judgements that make the play an exercise in sophistication. A version of the gull-knave relationship is used to expose the absurd vanity of an aspirant to the seasoned traveller's brand of knowingness. In Volpone's and Mosca's plot, however, all the gulls fancy themselves a jump ahead of the others and believe themselves knaves. Sir Pol is from his talk taken for a naive impostor, by circumstance supposed a clumsy knave, and finally by design made a gull. Peregrine is not a knave, but sophistication courts knavery when its first principle is that a man should not readily be taken in, and that he should be good at taking in others:

> Well, wise Sir Pol: since you have practised, thus,
> Upon my freshmanship, I'll try your salt-head,
> What proof it is against a counter-plot. (IV.iii, 22–4)

In Volpone's plot, the gulls are in the last phase taunted in turn for their failures of 'wisdom': Corbaccio (beard of 'grave length') is 'over-reached', Corvino ('traded in the world') is caught like the crow by the fox in the fable, and the skilled Voltore is left without a 'quirk to avoid gullage'. But the culpable innocence of Sir Pol is less offensive then the culpable guilt of the principal gulls; his punishment is correspondingly muted as he and his wife leave the Venetian clime and put to sea for 'physic'.[7]

The aptness of Peregrine's plot (and Jonson's) was to be nicely demonstrated some hundred and fifty years later when Lord Chesterfield played a similar trick on Montesquieu in Venice.[8] Following an argument about the precedence of French *esprit* and English common sense, Montesquieu returned from a sight-seeing round of Venice to find a badly dressed Frenchman waiting to warn him against meddling in Venetian affairs of state:

> '. . . Les Inquisiteurs d'État ont les yeux ouverts sur votre conduite, on vous épie, on suit tous vos pas, on tient note de tous vos projets, on ne doute point que vous n'écriviez. Je scais de science certaine qu'on doit, peut-être aujourd'huy, peut-être demain, faire chez vous une visite. Voyez, monsieur, si en effet vous avez écrit, et songez, qu'une ligne innocente, mais mal interprétée, vous coûteroit la vie.'

When Chesterfield called a little while later he found that Montesquieu had burnt his papers and made arrangements to leave Venice at three o'clock in the morning.

The Chesterfield story shows that Jonson's wit might alight upon any traveller who displays innocent curiosity about a city and goes

[7] For the nature of Lady Would-be's pretensions see note on page 76.

[8] The story is fully reported by Diderot in a letter to Sophie Volland, 5 September 1762. See Herford and Simpson Vol. IX, p. 728.

about taking notes, but also that the aspirant to political wisdom is particularly vulnerable. It suggests too a generality of application that discounts attempts to turn Sir Pol into a specific caricature. The most canvassed figure has been Sir Henry Wotton, British ambassador to Venice for most of the period 1604 to 1624, but the circumstance would mainly ensure that Wotton (who was a friend of Jonson's) would have been among the play's most amused spectators—he had more reason than most to know the extent and boundaries of Venetian political intrigue. It is not improbable, however, that Jonson did enjoy the occasional satirical glance at an acquaintance or public figure including perhaps Sir Antony Shirley, and even Wotton.[9] But there is a great difference between opportunities casually taken and systematic caricature.

Volpone, Mosca and the Classical Satirists

Although Venice supplies a good theatrical model for the acquisitive society devoted to the sanctities of gold, the play in so far as it is about legacy-hunters owes more to the satirists of Greece and Rome (particularly Lucian and Horace) and in so far as it is tragical satire it owes most to Juvenal. Legacy-hunting was a possible profession in ancient Greece, and is a favoured theme of the Greek New Comedy; in the Rome of Horace and Juvenal it is represented as a likely one; and in the later work of Lucian (writing in Athens) it is ubiquitous, and comes to the notice of the underworld where:[10]

> Pluto directs Hermes to bring him the fortune and legacy-hunters and flatterers of a certain rich man, and to suffer the latter to outlive his fawning satellites.

The idea is capable of much refinement—some to be found in Lucian's continuation in the *Dialogues of the Dead*, and more in Jonson's play where Volpone becomes, as it were, his own Pluto and affords for himself a kind of survival. If Volpone owes something of his wit and sense of justice to Lucian, he may also be imagined a reader of Horace's fifth Satire of Book II, which offers the metaphor of the gaping crow (I.ii, 97) together with a few more insights into the nature of fawning satellites. It is not merely whimsical so to imagine, for Volpone and Mosca are self-consciously literary—

[9] The claim that Wotton is specifically caricatured is fully developed by J. D. Rea in his edition of the play (1919). For the other possibilities see Herford and Simpson Vol. IX, pp. 681–2; like Gifford, however, they would rule out Sir Thomas Sutton the founder of the Charterhouse, who was said by Aubrey to be a model for Volpone himself.

[10] The argument of *Dialogues of the Dead* V is quoted from H. Williams's translation (1913). The next four dialogues are also relevant.

Mosca devises an allusive entertainment which Volpone appreciates, and Volpone can cite Sophocles in an attempt to hold his own with Lady Would-be's literary pretensions. The knaves are literate.

The most powerful strain in the play's satire upon the human condition (as distinct from its social satire) has its analogues, and sometimes its source, in Juvenal or in Pliny. Extracts from Juvenal's tenth Satire are given in the appendix, and it can readily be seen that frightening insights into human mutability and distress are deployed by Mosca both to witty acquisitive purpose and with searching moral irony. His reassurance to Corvino, for instance, that Volpone can hear nothing of their designs upon him, is serving the purpose of closing the trap upon another gull while testifying to the pathetic disintegration that waits for the 'real' Volpone, Mosca and Corvino alike:

He knows no man,
No face of friend, nor name of any servant,
Who 'twas that fed him last, or gave him drink:
Not those, he hath begotten, or brought up
Can he remember. (I.v, 39–43)

The exchange between Volpone and Mosca after Corbaccio has left them in Act I, Scene iv, has a greater *gravitas*. Mosca's servility acknowledges Volpone's 'grave instructions', and Volpone responds with wisdom acquired from Seneca and Pliny (both, as it happens, writers of the time of Claudius and Nero):

So many cares, so many maladies,
So many fears attending on old age,
Yea, death so often called on, as no wish
Can be more frequent with 'em, their limbs faint,
Their senses dull, their seeing, hearing, going,
All dead before them; yea, their very teeth,
Their instruments of eating, failing them:
Yet this is reckoned life! (I.iv, 144–51)

There is a touch of mockery and parody, as if Volpone were assuming the tragedian's role (this is indeed 'grave instruction'), but the sombre truths refuse to be carried lightly. Volpone can reconcile his contempt of life in old age with his determination to exhaust it in middle age; but the play, like age, will overtake him. His performance as a mountebank makes another contribution to our sense of the precariousness of the human state as he trades his 'sovereign and approved remedy' for:

the *mal caduco*, cramps, convulsions, paralyses, epilepsies, *tremor-cordia*, retired nerves, ill vapours of the spleen, stoppings of the liver, the stone, the strangury, *hernia ventosa*, *iliaca passio* . . . and . . . *melancholia hypocondriaca*. (II.ii, 103–8)

The marvellous energy, invention and confidence of the masquerade, however they challenge and foil human distress, cannot wholly subdue it—even momentarily in the vigour of the rhetoric. It is therefore fitting that the diseased state that he mimics should finally overtake him, at first symbolically:

MOSCA
But what, sir, if they ask
After the body?
VOLPONE
Say, it was corrupted.
MOSCA
I'll say it stunk, sir. (V.ii, 76–8)

and finally, literally:

And, since the most was gotten by imposture,
By feigning lame, gout, palsy, and such diseases,
Thou art to lie in prison, cramped with irons,
Till thou be'st sick, and lame indeed. (V.xii, 121–4)

His wealth will be 'confiscate to the Hospital, of the *Incurabili*', founded, as the more knowledgeable Venetian traveller would remember, for the treatment of venereal disease. Juvenal would have enjoyed the joke.

Mosca's learning (if we may so put it) is more miscellaneous than Volpone's; his analysis of the vices and weaknesses of lawyers (I.iii, 51–66) and physicians (I.iv, 20–35) is from the Renaissance Latin of Cornelius Agrippa, while his entertainment in Act I, Scene ii, snatches material from Lucian, Diogenes Laertius, and Erasmus. But again, the wisdom is tactically and perversely deployed while Jonson's irony plays upon it: the physician is mocked by knave and mountebank, and the advocate is enlisted in criminal imposture, but disease and the law will finally take their course.

The entertainment has been taken by some commentators to be a significant encapsulation of the play's theme, and it does indeed offer a curious gloss on the main action. Its deliberate *gaucherie* of manner, however, and its placing in the play as an aspect of Volpone's amusement at the antics of freaks, prevent it from being the vehicle of momentous truths that J. D. Rea and others would make it. In Lucian's *Dialogue of the Cobbler and the Cock* the cock is able to use the tale of Pythagoras's migrant soul to reconcile the cobbler to his poverty; Mosca uses it to suggest that the wisdom of Pythagoras is now (embodied in the hermaphrodite) a plaything of the rich. But, as A. B. Kernan points out, the changing roles and forms in the play are not only a source of entertainment for Volpone and Mosca, they are manifestations of a grim process that finally overtakes them. In so far as it idolises folly, the entertainment is rightly said to derive from Erasmus, but the debt is not profound; Jonson's debt in the play at large may be more so, but it cannot be adequately demonstrated from this scene alone.

'PURITY OF LANGUAGE'

Something has already been said, and much implied, about Jonson's poetic language. It might be seen as bringing Marlowe's energies under Horatian rule—a technical feat that corresponds to Jonson's readiness to subdue his sympathy with Renaissance aspirations to his respect for classical canons of good sense.

The phrase 'purity of language' may remind us that among the many pointless tensions expressed in the notorious war of the theatres, there is one that had a distinct significance and continues to animate the Epistle prefixed to *Volpone*: it is between those poets who are merely 'naturals' and 'contemners of all helps and arts', and those 'true artificers' whose 'divine instinct' is tempered by study and by labour. In its cruder forms the distinction looks like a simple one between the vulgar poet and the learned; but it is capable in Jonson's hands of much refinement, under the general maxim (from a Greek fragment) that 'without art, nature can never be perfect; and without nature art can claim no being.'[11]

The Epistle expresses disgust for those who write 'with such impropriety of phrase, such dearth of sense, so bold prolepses, so racked metaphors'. Jonson was probably thinking of Marston (much of the Epistle repeats material from the Apologetical Dialogue appended to the *Poetaster*) but he could also be anticipating Dr Johnson's Augustan judgement upon Shakespeare's style—'ungrammatical, perplexed and obscure'.

Jonson's dramatic poetry is often graphic where Shakespeare's is evocative, clear where Shakespeare is elusive, explicit where Shakespeare is mysterious. Volpone, for example, characterises the ruthlessness of society with clarity, gaiety and rigour:

> I use no trade, no venture;
> I wound no earth with ploughshares; fat no beasts
> To feed the shambles; have no mills for iron,
> Oil, corn, or men, to grind 'em into poulder. (I.i, 33–6)

There are metaphors here—the wounded earth, the feeding of the slaughterhouse and the grinding of men to powder, but they are so immediately related to the phenomena they touch that they strike with almost literal force; it would not be surprising if Jonson meant the 'men' to be raw material for bone-meal or mummia. When

[11] See *Timber or Discoveries*, section cxxx.

Shakespeare's Pericles expresses his sense of human tyranny in Antioch, the boundaries of the metaphor are much less clear:

> The blind mole casts
> Copp'd hills towards heaven, to tell the earth is throng'd
> By man's oppression; and the poor worm doth die for't.
> (*Pericles* I.i, 99–101)

Jonson could not have invented a metaphor whose implications are so hard to contain; the mole seems to have been driven from the earth's surface and therefore blinded 'by man's oppression', its hills are a signal of protest towards heaven—and yet it too is an oppressor, a killer of worms. Shakespeare's metaphor obscurely suggests that oppression, protest and suffering are laws of the natural and human worlds. Jonson might well have found it 'racked'.

Other comparisons might be made with Shakespeare to similar purpose, between Isabella's resistance to Angelo in *Measure for Measure* and Celia's to Volpone, or between the Duke's contempt of life in that play (III.i, 5–40) and Volpone's (I.iv, 144–59), and almost every page of Shakespeare offers metaphors that Jonson would have thought indecorous. But decorum in Jonson's art is not merely a principle by which words are judged acceptable to polite taste; it is an energising force requiring that every word should meet in context the demands made upon it:

> For a man to write well, there are required three necessaries—to read the best authors, observe the best speakers, and much exercise of his own style. In style, to consider what ought to be written, and after what manner, he must first think and excogitate his matter, then choose his words, and examine the weight of either. Then take care, in placing and ranking both matter and words, that the composition be comely; and to do this with diligence and often. No matter how slow the style be at first, so it be laboured and accurate; seek the best, and be not glad of the forward conceits, or first words, that offer themselves to us; but judge of what we invent, and order what we approve. Repeat often what we have formerly written; which beside that it helps the consequence, and makes the juncture better, it quickens the heat of imagination, that often cools in the time of setting down, and gives it new strength, as if it grew lustier by going back. (*Timber or Discoveries* cxv)

Jonson's labour and accuracy confers in the end an astonishing swiftness and power of movement. Voltore's speeches to the Scrutineo, for example, are totally composed of forensic skill and forensic pathos; the rhetoric is absolute, there are no expressions or cadences that do not wholly belong to it, for the 'invention' has been scrupulously judged:

> And, as for them, I will conclude with this,
> That vicious persons when they are hot, and fleshed
> In impious acts, their constancy abounds:
> Damned deeds are done with greatest confidence.
> (IV.vi, 50–3)

The staggering cheek of the closing thought perfects Voltore's malicious fantasy. It is one of the delights of Jonson's art that fantasies are splendidly articulated, whether Voltore's of righteous indignation, or Volpone's of sensual prodigality and golden dissolution:

> See, here, a rope of pearl; and each, more orient
> Than that the brave Egyptian queen caroused:
> Dissolve, and drink 'em. See, a carbuncle,
> May put out both the eyes of our St. Mark;
> A diamant, would have bought Lollia Paulina,
> When she came in, like star-light, hid with jewels,
> That were the spoils of provinces . . . (III.vii, 191–7)

The allusions to Cleopatra and to Lollia Paulina exemplify the contribution that creative imitation makes to the play, for Jonson borrows both notions of heroic indulgence from Pliny (*Natural History* ix, lviii). But the sail of the verse (reminding us that Jonson honoured Marlowe for his mighty line) confers a grace and insolence upon 'the spoils of provinces' not to be found in the matter-of-fact of Pliny's prose, although the phrase itself is translated precisely (*provinciarum scilicet spoliis pratae*).

The arts of imitation and allusion are not, as Jonson uses them, parasitic—they renew the life of the imagination both in the past and in the present. As he himself puts it, the first requisites in a poet are 'natural wit' and 'exercise' while the third is:

> imitation, *imitatio*, to be able to convert the substance or riches of another poet to his own use. To make choice of one excellent man above the rest, and so to follow him till he grow very he, or so like him as the copy may be mistaken for the principal. Not as a creature that swallows what it takes in, crude, raw, or undigested; but that feeds with an appetite, and hath a stomach to concoct, divide, and turn all into nourishment. (*Timber or Discoveries* cxxx)

With this in mind one may browse with greater satisfaction in the literature that the play calls into service, finding (for example) that the voices of Horace and Juvenal can be heard the more clearly because Jonson had attended to them.

'THE MANNERS OF THE SCENE'

Jonson studied the theatrical art of the past as exactingly as he did its poetry, but both as playwright and as poet he made contributions decisively new. We have noticed that the conventions of Classical Comedy meet those of Tudor Interlude, and, it may be added, of the *commedia dell'arte*; brought to Jonson's forge and file (his favourite metaphors for the poet's craft) they are fashioned into a fabric at once massively and sensitively wrought. The debt to classical comedy has been sufficiently indicated—the gull-and-knave structure, the antics of the witty parasite, the satire upon professional men, the legacy-hunting motif, all have their beginnings in Greece and Rome. Medieval and Tudor plays, on the other hand, supply something of the moral design; the Devil and his acolytes (Dissimulation, Ambidexter, Hypocrisy) are still recognisable in Volpone and Mosca, while Volpone as seducer and tempter might be seen as in a different line from Satan in Eden or in the wilderness. Thus the spectacle of Mosca exposing at once the physical and the moral frailties of Corbaccio in Act I, Scene iv, might have satisfied a Roman audience or a medieval English one.

The Venetian scene made it appropriate if not prerequisite that the play should pay its respects to the *commedia dell'arte*. In part indeed it offers the *commedia* documentary recognition, as when Corvino calls Volpone's Scoto 'Flaminio', Celia 'Franciscina' and himself by the name of the stock cuckold 'Pantalone di Besogniosi', or when Volpone makes Nano his Zany and styles him Zan Fritada. More significantly, however, Italian comedy styles leave their mark on the manners and mood of the play as a whole. The play is not an improvisation but it often wins the best effects associated with improvisation; it is not a masked comedy (to name another Italian type) but it often works in the same way; it has no pantomime, but acted in silence its spectacle might still be made entertaining and significant.

The qualities of the play as emblematic spectacle owe much to its assimilation of beast fable, from Aesop or from popular lore:[12]

> vulture, kite,
> Raven, and gor-crow, all my birds of prey,
> That think me turning carcass, now they come.
> I am not for 'em yet.
> . . . . not a fox
> Stretched on the earth, with fine delusive sleights,
> Mocking a gaping crow? (I.ii, 89–92, 95–7)

Sir Pol is a chattering parrot, and so is his wife; Peregrine is a pilgrim

[12] See J. A. Barish, 'The Double Plot in *Volpone*', *Modern Philology* I. I. (1953), 83–92; reprinted in *Ben Jonson* (Twentieth Century Views) ed. Barish, 1963. See also D. A. Scheve, 'Traditional Fox Lore and Volpone', *Review of English Studies*, 1950, and H. Levin, 'Jonson's Metempsychosis', *Philological Quarterly*, 1943.

hawk, and the hawk (by one of Jonson's epigrams) 'pursues the truth, strikes at ignorance, and makes the fool its quarry'. Ape, ass, crocodile, mule, gennet, wolf and chameleon all have a place in Jonson's vision of human predatoriness and folly, and assist in the impression that men readily lapse into beasts and lose their distinctive manliness or virtue. Volpone's attendant grotesques—dwarf, eunuch and hermaphrodite—take on the same significance, like the rout of Comus.

Dominating the play, however, is the fox's capacity to deceive the bird of prey; it is related to the skill by which a man imposes himself on another by flattery, and therefore to all modes of deception and false appearance. There is wit in deception and there is a glory in changing shapes. Again the spectacle does much to sustain the sequence of metamorphoses—from the doctoring of Volpone's face on the stage to the prodding of the vast tortoise-shell that conceals Sir Politic. Characters and situations change appearance with exhilarating and bewildering pace until all human identities are disfigured, all relationships confused, and the truth made inaccessible to reason and law. Final disintegration threatens when the fourth Avocatore moves to match Mosca with his daughter; but within moments Venetian order is resumed with the judicial cry 'Disrobe that parasite!' The conventional comic servant discarding his master's robes becomes the symbol of Venice restored to its 'honoured fathers'—at least for the time being.

'GENTLE AFFECTIONS'

It may seem among the more surprising claims that Jonson makes for the comic poet that he should 'stir up gentle affections', for *Volpone* has not infrequently been thought sombre, grim and even 'cynical'.[13] 'Cynical' has become a carelessly used word of imprecise meaning, but since Crates (a true Cynic) is mentioned in Mosca's entertainment, it is worth remarking that the play at large cannot be regarded as cynical in the strict sense, for it does not recommend that man discard his civilised pretensions and return to his animal simplicity. On the contrary, it commends the virtues—of wit, generosity and vitality—that Volpone and Mosca both embody and pervert; it persuades us that fine energies and impulses are running into strange forms or running to waste; that reverence, bounty, love and ceremony exist still and that the English language is ripe for their expression when they return to their proper shapes. 'Gentle

[13] See Edmund Wilson, 'Morose Ben Jonson', in *Ben Jonson* (Twentieth Century Views) ed. Barish. Wilson is not strictly concerned with Jonson's cynicism but his 'anal eroticism', which he related to the avarice and sadism of Jonson's heroes and to the pedantry and arrogance of Jonson himself.

affections' in Jonson's critical dialect does not mean merely 'tenderness of regard' but, more fully, 'noble dispositions of feeling', and these are stirred up less by our immediate sympathy with Bonario and Celia (although that is surely present) than by our freshened insight into the nature of imposture and the precariousness of civilised values. Whoever jeers at that last commonplace, stands in Mosca's shoes.

THE PLAY ON THE STAGE

The title page of the Folio tells us that *Volpone* was acted by the King's Men in the year 1605, which by the court calendar would mean between 1 March 1605 and 1 March 1606. If the reports of whale and porpoise in the Thames, however, refer to the actual events of late January 1606 (see II.i, 40n., 46) then the most probable date for the staging of the play at the Globe is some time in February. The Dedicatory Epistle implies that performances were later given at Oxford and Cambridge, probably in the summer of 1606.

The play is manifestly well fitted for performance in either public theatre or private hall, being rich in effects both broad and intimate. Its mode of production and its use of stage architecture and furniture would, of course, differ according to circumstance. It is an advantage in reading the play, however, to postulate the existence of upper stage areas (a gallery and perhaps a window-stage) together with a central structure serving to enclose Volpone's bed in the home scenes and the judicial bench in the Scrutineo, while readily conforming with the street architecture in the outdoor scenes.[14] The Brussels stage illustrated in fig. 2 suggests one possibility; with a more open and usable gallery the upper part of the structure would be superfluous, leaving a pavilion or canopy stage of the size of a large four-poster bed.

The action may be regarded as observing a rhythm between formal scenes with a strong centre accent, in which the gold, the bed or the judicial chair commands attention, and scenes of freer movement across the platform in front of the street façade.[15] A Jacobean audience would readily have accepted a range of conventions still promptly intelligible to a modern audience, by which the scene may be supposed changed when all the players leave the stage and some return

[14] The most useful account of the Elizabethan and Jacobean playhouses is C. Walter Hodges, *The Globe Restored*, 1953.

[15] The distinction made here between centre and side accent is owed to G. R. Kernodle, *From Art to Theatre*, 1947, but I would wish to extend it from a principle of spectacle to a general principle of performance and production.

Figure 2

after a short interval, and which normally assumes the setting to be indoors with the canopy curtains open and outdoors with them closed.

With the furniture suggested, and the conventions regarded, the rhythm of the action can be observed without fuss. The canopy curtains would be open on Volpone's bed in the first scene, with the 'shrine' of treasure discovered above and behind it; the bed need be no more than rich cushions on a platform together with hangings either from the centre or from the fringe of the canopy.

The second Act opens before Corvino's house, when the curtains might be drawn, allowing the canopy to take its place like a window or doorway in the façade. The mountebank stage would be erected by the troop in the minute or two before Volpone enters (the structure illustrated in fig. 3 looks frail but its front supports might be hinged and its back ones morticed, with iron braces at each corner). Celia's window might be either a window-stage or the gallery—she must be in a position to throw 'down' her handkerchief. Scene iv of Act II, described by Gifford and subsequent editors as in 'Volpone's House', may in fact be unlocated and played before curtains still

Figure 3

drawn. They might be opened for the remaining scenes of the Act (but with the treasure concealed and cushions removed) to signify the interior of Corvino's house.

Act III is complicated by the need to provide hiding places for Bonario, and temporarily to shield Volpone from view. Its first two scenes are unlocated 'street' scenes; the next three are in Volpone's house and need the bed to be dominant, even when it is not the centre of the action. Volpone himself apparently draws the curtains at the end of Act III, Scene v, but these could be bed-hangings as distinct from the main drapes of the canopy. Mosca hides Bonario in Act III, Scene vi, perhaps behind the 'traverse' which is mentioned in a later direction (V.iii, 8), and which might hang across one arch of an arcaded stage or across a door not in use. Bonario is subsequently invited by Mosca to withdraw to the gallery, which may happen in fact or only by gesture, according to the theatre's resources. The Folio leaves an awkwardness at this point (III.vii, 15–72) for it neither gives sufficient reason for Mosca to leave the stage nor gives him work to do on it. A. B. Kernan adds the direction 'Returns to Volpone's couch, opens the curtains, and whispers to him', which is an apt solution, with the whispering becoming audible at line 68. Otherwise Mosca and Volpone can be represented as listening to Corvino and Celia from their place of concealment in the canopy; Volpone's delighted exclamation then refers to the degrading spectacle that Corvino is presenting. Towards the end of the scene Bonario 'leaps out from where Mosca had placed him'; this could be from the gallery itself (an athletic feat), or he could watch from the gallery, come down unseen, and appear from behind the traverse.

Act IV starts with three unlocated street scenes with the pavilion curtains drawn, but they may open for the remaining scenes to allow the structure to become the judicial seat of the first Avocatore in the Scrutineo.

In the fifth Act the canopy perhaps serves again as Volpone's bed in the first scene, but its dominant function is as setting for another display of Volpone's wealth as Mosca takes its inventory. Volpone's hiding place behind the traverse (which can mean 'screen' as well as 'curtain') would be to one side, while Mosca prevails over gold and gulls from the centre. Scene iv is at Sir Politic's house, but whether in a courtyard or an ante-room is not clear—Peregrine is not apparently admitted to the house, but the merchants 'knock without' at line 47. The canopy stage could serve for Sir Politic's study, and his papers could be burned there as the merchants rush in. Scene v, which is editorially at Volpone's house, need not be localised, and the curtains can remain closed, to open again for the final scenes of justice.

Costume and Setting

For the general visual impression of the play Mario Praz has made comparisons with Titian, with his portrait of Aretino ('diabolical', 'thrilled by the soul's degradation') and his *mascarone* ('we are in the presence of the same audacious and malignant buffoonery').[16] But for relevant, if rather early, visual impressions of Venice—its costume and architecture—Carpaccio remains the best source for the producer. The extracts from Coryat's *Crudities* given in the appendix may also be found to assist in making the spectacle of the play both accurate and eloquent.

Music

The most famous song of the play, *Come, my Celia*, was set to music by Ferrabosco and included in his *Book of Ayres*. A facsimile, together with commentary on other aspects of the music of *Volpone*, is included in Willa McClung Evans, *Ben Jonson and Elizabethan Music* (revised edition 1965). See also F. W. Sternfeld, 'Song in

[16] Mario Praz, *The Flaming Heart*, 1958, p. 183.

Jonson's Comedy: A Gloss on *Volpone*' in *Studies in the English Renaissance Drama*, ed. J. W. Bennett and others, 1959, pp. 310–21.

A Note on Stage History

Volpone was one of the few Jacobean plays to continue to hold the stage in Pepys's time, but by the beginning of the eighteenth century it was in decline; as one writer put it, '*The Mourning Bride*, *Plain Dealer*, *Volpone*, or *Tamerlane*, will hardly fetch us a tolerable audience, unless we stuff the bills with long entertainments of dances, songs, scaramouched entries, and what not.'[17] It seems to have been neglected in the nineteenth century, but was revived in the twentieth with a great performance by Baliol Holloway (Volpone) and Ion Swinley (Mosca) at the Lyric Theatre Hammersmith in 1921. Among more recent performances the most notable was Donald Wolfit's with the Advance Players in 1947. A distinguished French film has been made after Stefan Zweig's German adaptation of the play; in it Mosca is left in command of Volpone's wealth—ready to spend it—and Volpone is outcast, being officially dead and buried.

THE TEXT AND ITS PRESENTATION

Dr Johnson did well to remark of textual scholars and their craft that where the matter to be investigated is so near to inexistence, its bulk must be enlarged by rage and exclamation. For disputes about the text of *Volpone*—where the points at issue are more than usually trivial—have been uncommonly acrimonious.

The history begins auspiciously, for two admirable, but not impeccable, texts were published in Jonson's lifetime, apparently with his authority and collaboration: the 1607 Quarto, *Volpone or the Foxe*, printed for Thomas Thorpe by an unknown printer; and the version in the great Folio of *Works* printed and published by William Stansby in 1616. Between the Quarto and Folio texts of certain other Jonson plays there are marked discrepancies, but the Folio *Volpone* is almost slavishly faithful to the Quarto, with manifestly purposeful departures or additions numbering only about one hundred.[18]

[17] Quoted from Malcolm Elwin, *The Playgoer's Handbook to Restoration Drama*, 1928, p. 159.

[18] De Vocht, in his edition of the Quarto, estimates 3175 alterations of the Q text in F, but the great majority are trivially typographical; he counts 83 emendations; see de Vocht pp. 245–6.

Editorial opinion, however, is divided about the extent to which Jonson himself undertook the detailed work of seeing both the Quarto and the Folio texts through the press. Herford and Simpson ascribe to Jonson the twenty-one press corrections they locate in seven copies of the Quarto, thereby allowing the Quarto a very considerable authority;[19] but they also believe that Jonson himself 'carefully corrected' the copy of the Quarto from which the Folio was set up, and they would therefore give the Folio a still greater authority.[20] Henry de Vocht, on the other hand, finds no sufficient reason to believe Jonson responsible for the 'corrections' embodied in the Folio; he finds them uneven in quality and attributes them to a reader or readers employed by Stansby. In an analysis at once conscientious and tendentious, he concludes that the Quarto better represents Jonson's intentions but that it too has its burdens of errors, and that Jonson was not therefore responsible for its detailed supervision and its press-corrections.[21]

In practice it seems wise to make use of both texts. Herford and Simpson themselves enlist the Quarto even when seeking to print the Folio *literatim*,[22] while de Vocht acknowledges the superiority of the Folio where it corrects what he calls 'obvious misprints'.[23]

The present edition is based on the following assumptions: (1) that Q is a conscientious attempt to print a manuscript that Jonson had prepared for publication; (2) that there is no evidence for supposing Jonson personally responsible for the Q press-corrections; (3) that Jonson read and marked a copy of Q for the use of the F printers, but, finding the text generally satisfactory, his interventions were few and unsystematic. I do not think any of these propositions can be decisively proved, but they would account for the superiority of Q in certain details of punctuation and presentation, while allowing the Folio 'corrections' to be treated with full respect. They make it unnecessary to arbitrate between the advocates of the total authority of either text. Each text may be right in any particular instance, but judgement begins with a prejudice in favour of the accidentals of the Quarto and the substantive readings of the Folio; it is also possible that both may be wrong.

[19] See Herford and Simpson Vol. V, p. 7.

[20] Herford and Simpson Vol. V, p. 8.

[21] For comment on de Vocht's argument see Herford and Simpson Vol. IX, pp. 74–86; de Vocht's case is not wholly answered, but many of its weaknesses are displayed.

[22] e.g. at II.vi, 15, III.iii, 5, III.iv, 79, III.vii, 133.

[23] He lists two dozen under this description (p. 143) and allows a number of minor corrections elsewhere (e.g. p. 135).

Spelling and Word-forms

This is a modern-spelling text which therefore eludes many problems of orthographic interpretation between Quarto and Folio. Every attempt to modernise, however, without deforming the text, brings its crop of compromises and anomalies, and this is no exception. I have silently regularised such forms as 'then' for 'than', where the sense requires it, 'off' for 'of', and 'wives' for 'wife's'. Other preferred forms include:

advices (for advises)
carat (for caract)
chequeen (for cecchine)
commendatore (for commandadore)
endure (for indure)
illustrious (for illustrous)
ostrich (for estrich)
travel (for travail, where the sense requires)
valour (for valure, where the sense requires)
venture (for venter, where the sense requires)
window (for windore)

A few old forms, however, have been retained to mark Jonson's occasionally resolute conservatism:

diamant (diamond); a Middle English form that Jonson preferred.
half-perth (ha'p'orth)
moyle (mule); at I.ii, 39 and 41, where it is deliberately quaint; Jonson's 'mule' is retained at V.ix, 9.
porcpisces (porpoise); Jonson liked to preserve the etymology.
poulder (powder); again for its etymology.
splendidous (splendid); retained for its greater sonority.
venting (vending); a distinct word (now obsolete) that Jonson preferred.

A number of participle forms have been modernised (e.g. 'kissed' for 'kist') and 'shew' has throughout been rendered as 'show'.

Punctuation

The punctuation of both Q and F may be said largely to conform to Jonson's principles and practice, as manifest in other texts and declared in his *Grammar*. It tends to display as fully as possible the grammatical elements of each clause and sentence, and to regulate the movement of the syntax with a high degree of precision. By modern conventions the pointing is heavy, but once its functions are recognised, it does not obstruct reading but rather adds to its definition and clarity.

A comma in Jonson does not require a pause, but it gives the interpreting actor opportunity for one. For example, these lines of Mosca to Voltore are capable of a choice of renderings:

> You still are, what you were, sir. Only you,
> Of all the rest, are he, commands his love:
> And you do wisely, to preserve it, thus,
> With early visitation, and kind notes
> Of your good meaning to him, which, I know,
> Cannot but come most grateful. (I.iii, 1–6)

The first sentence may be spoken as if it were free from commas, allowing them merely to mark the grammatical structure ('what you were' being a subordinate clause); but if the pauses are observed, the clause begins to sound ironic and equivocal, as if Mosca hesitates to say what Voltore really is. Similarly, observing the pause after 'he' gives a particular force to 'commands', but the reader or actor is not bound to observe it. Again, a pause after 'preserve it' and after 'thus', would enable Mosca to make the gift of the plate more important than the visitation. Mosca's subtle rhetoric, therefore, is well served by this mode of punctuation; although it remains vital not to over-interpret, but to allow easy and rapid movement over the commas when occasion requires.

In the passage quoted above, the words 'Of all the rest' are enclosed in brackets in Q and F. Where modern practice allows three parenthesising devices—commas, brackets and dashes, Jonson was apt to use only the last two. This edition substitutes commas for brackets for the more open kind of parenthesis, where there is only a slight diversion from the run of the thought; but Jonson's brackets are retained when they enclose a secondary or supplementary observation:

> No, sir, on visitation:
> (I'll tell you how, anon) and, staying long,
> The youth, he grows impatient, rushes forth. (III.ix, 45–7)

Dashes are retained where they occur, and are occasionally substituted for Jonson's brackets—particularly in asides and interruptions.

In both texts Jonson makes lavish use of semi-colons and colons, often where modern practice would call for a full stop. These have been retained unless they fall at the end of speeches, or of interjections or commands, when stops or exclamation marks are substituted. The colon in Jonson often expresses the climax of a movement of thought, featuring the clause or sentence that follows:

> He knows no man,
> No face of friend, nor name of any servant,
> Who 'twas that fed him last, or gave him drink:

Not those, he hath begotten, or brought up
Can he remember. (I.v, 39–43)

Reported speech has been cast into quotation marks, and queries and exclamation marks have sometimes been changed to conform to modern usage. A number of commas have been silently deleted where they cause awkwardness or misunderstanding without performing an expressive function. For example, some commas have been dropped from these lines, sampled from Act I, Scene v, of the Folio:

I still interpreted the nods, he made
(Through weakenesse) for consent: (35–6)

Faith, I could stifle him, rarely, with a pillow,
As well, as any woman, that should keep him. (68–9)

VOLPONE Not, now.
Some three hours, hence—
MOSCA I told the squire, so much. (98)

Elsewhere, a very few commas have been added to secure consistency (which Jonson himself sought) in the presentation of some phrases (e.g. 'Pray you,') and forms of address (e.g. 'Sir,'). The edition remains, however, as conservative of the Quarto and Folio punctuation as the circumstances of a modernised text permit.

Stage Directions

The Quarto is without stage-directions but the Folio adds twenty-nine, usually of an innocent if superfluous character—indicating knocking at the door, Celia's casting her handkerchief from the window, Volpone peeping from behind a traverse, etc. I share de Vocht's view that the directions are either unnecessary or inadequate, and I do not think they can be confidently attributed to Jonson. On the other hand, they cannot plausibly be ascribed to anyone else, and it seems likely that he at least tolerated them, as he might otherwise have had them removed from the Folio margins. It would be possible to speculate about the publisher, William Stansby, himself reading and annotating the Quarto that Jonson had marked, or was to mark, for the press; but there is no sufficient evidence, and to set aside the directions would be an impertinence.

The Folio directions have been retained, but transferred from the margins into the body of the text; where they are likely to be confused with the text they are enclosed in round brackets. In both Q and F the names of characters playing in a scene are listed together at its head, without indication in the text of specific entrances and exits; these indications, together with other editorial directions (often derived from the 1640 Folio and from Gifford's 1816 edition), are enclosed in square brackets.

Quarto and Folio Variants

All verbal variants (i.e. those affecting the choice of form of a word) are recorded in the appended list, and most of them also in the page-notes. Only a selection of punctuation variants is included, however, to indicate the nature of the relationship between the two texts, and to enable the reader in special instances to make his own choice.[24]

Act and Scene Divisions

The Act and scene divisions, common to Q and F, are retained except for the correction of some errors in numbering. They often bring no break in the action, but with the entrance of major characters, they usually signify a turn of events.

[24] See below pp. 169–70.

A NOTE ON THE NOTES

THROUGHOUT the notes this edition is indebted to those that others have prepared: William Gifford (1816), W. Bang (1908), J. D. Rea (1919), Herford and Simpson (1937, 1950), Henry de Vocht (1937), David Cook (1962) and Alvin B. Kernan (1962). The scope of the edition does not permit more than a very few specific acknowledgements, but the reader who wishes for fuller information on contemporary and literary allusions will usually find it in Herford and Simpson Vol. IX (1950). There is little here that is original; the aim has been the more modest one of relevance and economy.

Since so many words have called for both lexical gloss and comment, there has been no attempt to discriminate the two kinds by a line across the foot-notes (as used in some other plays of the series); a line is only used for the convenience of isolating the few very long notes.

Paraphrase and gloss should not, of course, be taken as full equivalents of the words annotated. Where, for example, 'forged practice' is glossed as 'contrived plot' (IV.v, 85), 'baited' as 'enticed' (IV.v, 146), and 'fleshed' as 'inured' (IV.vi, 51), the limited equivalences of meaning should not be allowed to mask the crucial differences of effect and energy. Many of the glosses are from the Oxford English Dictionary which, indeed, makes a better companion to the play than most commentators. Inverted commas enclose a gloss in which a meaning is indirectly rendered or paraphrased. No attempt has been made at total consistency in the glosses: some equivalents can be substituted in context for the glossed word, and others cannot; some words are glossed twice (because unlikely to be remembered), others at their first appearance only; and the Latin root of a word is given only when it is of particular relevance.

ACKNOWLEDGEMENTS

MY LARGE DEBT is to the comprehensive work of C. H. Herford and Percy and Evelyn Simpson, to the textual analysis of the Quarto offered by Henry de Vocht, and to editors of modernised texts from William Gifford (1816) to A. B. Kernan (1962). Some other specific acknowledgements are made in the notes, but I am aware of their inadequacy and am confident that they will not be mistaken for the sum of my obligations. My colleagues Dr Brian Morris, Dr Brian Gibbons, Mr Bob Jones and Mr Bernard Harris have generously contributed facts and ideas; if I have not always enlisted them in the service of truth, the fault is not theirs. I am grateful to Mr David Crease who made the drawing for Figure 1.

The section on 'The Author' in the introduction is from Professor W. F. Bolton's edition of *Sejanus*.

FURTHER READING

Editions

Ben Jonson, ed. C. H. Herford, Percy Simpson and Evelyn Simpson, 11 vols., 1925–52. The standard edition.

Volpone, ed. J. D. Rea, Yale Studies in English 59, 1919. Valuable on the allusions and classical analogues of the play.

Volpone, ed. Henry de Vocht, Materials for the Study of the Old English Drama, 1937. The Quarto text with full apparatus.

Criticism

Barish, J. A., *Ben Jonson and the Language of Prose Comedy*, 1960.

Barish, J. A., ed., *Ben Jonson: A Collection of Critical Essays* (Twentieth Century Views), 1963.

Eliot, T. S., 'Ben Jonson', reprinted in *Elizabethan Dramatists*, 1963.

Ellis-Fermor, U., *The Jacobean Drama* (fourth edition with additional material, 1961).

Gilbert, A. H., *The Symbolic Persons in the Masques of Ben Jonson*, 1948.

Knights, L. C., *Drama and Society in the Age of Jonson*, 1937.

Knoll, R. E., *Ben Jonson's Plays: An Introduction*, 1964.

Partridge, E. B., *The Broken Compass, A Study of the Major Comedies of Ben Jonson.*

Sackton, A. E., *Rhetoric as a Dramatic Language in Ben Jonson*, 1948.

Thayer, C. G., *Ben Jonson: Studies in the Plays*, 1963.

VOLPONE, OR THE FOXE.

A Comœdie.

Acted in the yeere 1605. By
the K. MAIESTIES
SERVANTS.

The Author B. I.

HORAT.
Simul & iucunda, & idonea dicere vitæ.

LONDON,
Printed by WILLIAM STANSBY.

M. DC. XVI.

BEN: IONSON

his

VOLPONE

Or

THE FOXE.

—*Simul & iucunda, & idonea dicere vitæ.*

Printed for *Thomas Thorppe.*
1607.

TO

THE MOST NOBLE AND MOST EQVALL SISTERS

THE TWO FAMOVS

VNIVERSITIES

FOR THEIR LOVE

AND

ACCEPTANCE

SHEW'N TO HIS POEME IN THE

PRESENTATION

BEN. IONSON

THE GRATEFVLL ACKNOWLEDGER

DEDICATES

BOTH IT AND HIMSELFE.

THE EPISTLE

Never (most equal Sisters) had any man a wit so presently excellent, as that it could raise itself; but there must come both matter, occasion, commenders, and favourers to it: if this be true, and that the fortune of all writers doth daily prove it, it behoves the careful to provide, well, towards these accidents; 5
and, having acquired them, to preserve that part of reputation most tenderly, wherein the benefit of a friend is also defended. Hence is it, that I now render myself grateful, and am studious to justify the bounty of your act: to which, though your mere authority were satisfying, yet, it being an age, wherein *Poetry*, 10
and the professors of it hear so ill, on all sides, there will a reason be looked for in the subject. It is certain, nor can it with any forehead be opposed, that the too-much licence of *Poetasters*, in this time, hath much deformed their mistress; that, every day, their manifold, and manifest ignorance, doth 15
stick unnatural reproaches upon her: but for their petulancy, it were an act of the greatest injustice, either to let the learned suffer; or so divine a skill (which indeed should not be attempted with unclean hands) to fall, under the least contempt. For,

1 *equal* in merit, in justice (Latin *aequus*), and perhaps in rivalry
1 *wit* talent
1 *presently* instantly
4 *that* i.e. 'that it be so'
5 *accidents* chances, secondary attributes
7 *benefit . . . friend* i.e. the good of the universities
11 *professors* practitioners
11 *hear so ill* are spoken so ill of (Latin *tam male audiunt*)
12 *subject* i.e. poetry (it must justify itself)
13 *forehead* confidence, countenance
14 *Poetasters* 'a petty or paltry poet' (*OED*)
16 *for* because of
16 *petulancy* rudeness, insolence

The Epistle. The so-called War of the Theatres in which Jonson's principal opponents were Dekker and Marston had virtually ended in 1604, when Jonson and Dekker collaborated in a Coronation Entertainment, and Marston dedicated his *Malcontent* to Jonson ('*Poetae Elegantissimo Gravissimo*'). The present Epistle, however, takes over material from the *Apologetical Dialogue* which was once spoken on the stage and was intended for inclusion in the 1602 edition of *Poetaster*—hence some surviving acerbities of tone. The critical principles of the Epistle are touched on in the Introduction.

if men will impartially, and not asquint, look toward the offices, and function of a Poet, they will easily conclude to themselves, the impossibility of any man's being a good Poet, without first being a good man. He that is said to be able to inform young men to all good disciplines, inflame grown men to all great virtues, keep old men in their best and supreme state, or as they decline to childhood, recover them to their first strength; that comes forth the interpreter, and arbiter of nature, a teacher of things divine, no less than human, a master in manners; and can alone (or with a few) effect the business of mankind: this, I take him, is no subject for pride, and ignorance to exercise their railing rhetoric upon. But, it will here be hastily answered, that the writers of these days are other things; that, not only their manners, but their natures are inverted; and nothing remaining with them of the dignity of Poet, but the abused name, which every scribe usurps: that now, especially in *dramatic*, or (as they term it) *stage poetry*, nothing but ribaldry, profanation, blasphemy, all licence of offence to God, and man, is practised. I dare not deny a great part of this (and am sorry, I dare not) because in some men's abortive features (and would they had never boasted the light) it is over-true: but, that all are embarked in this bold adventure for hell, is a most uncharitable thought, and, uttered, a more malicious slander. For my particular, I can (and from a most clear conscience) affirm, that I have ever trembled to think toward the least profaneness; have loathed the use of such foul, and unwashed bawdry, as is now made the food of the *scene*. And, howsoever I cannot escape, from some, the imputation of sharpness, but that they will say, I have taken a pride, or lust, to be bitter, and not my youngest infant but hath come into the world with all his teeth; I would ask of these supercilious politics, what nation, society, or general order, or state I have provoked? What public person? Whether I have not (in all these) preserved their dignity, as mine own person, safe? My works are read, allowed (I speak of those that are entirely mine) —look into them: what broad reproofs have I used? Where have I been particular? Where personal? except to a mimic, cheater, bawd, or buffoon—creatures (for their insolencies)

24 *inform* shape
29 *business* proper functions
40 *abortive features* miscarried creations—bad plays
49 *youngest infant* i.e. latest play—*Sejanus*
50–51 *politics* contrivers
55 *broad* licentious
56 *mimic* actor, imitator

worthy to be taxed? Yet, to which of these so pointingly, as he might not, either ingenuously have confessed, or wisely dissembled his disease? But it is not rumour can make men guilty, 60 much less entitle me, to other men's crimes. I know, that nothing can be so innocently writ, or carried, but may be made obnoxious to construction; marry, whilst I bear mine innocence about me, I fear it not. Application is now grown a trade with many; and there are, that profess to have a key for the 65 deciphering of everything: but let wise and noble persons take heed how they be too credulous, or give leave to these invading interpreters, to be over-familiar with their fames, who cunningly, and often, utter their own virulent malice, under other men's simplest meanings. As for those, that will (by faults 70 which charity hath raked up, or common honesty concealed) make themselves a name with the multitude, or (to draw their rude, and beastly claps) care not whose living faces they intrench, with their petulant styles; may they do it, without a rival, for me: I choose rather to live graved in obscurity, than 75 share with them, in so preposterous a fame. Nor can I blame the wishes of those severe, and wiser patriots, who, providing the hurts these licentious spirits may do in a state, desire rather to see fools, and devils, and those antique relics of barbarism retrieved, with all other ridiculous and exploded 80 follies: than behold the wounds of private men, of princes, and nations. For, as Horace makes Trebatius speak, among these,

—Sibi quisque timet, quamquam est intactus, et odit.

58 *taxed* censured 58 *Yet* F (Q Or)
59 *ingenuously* F (Q ingeniously) evidently a correction
62 *carried* conducted
62–63 *made . . . construction* 'made harmful by misinterpretation' or 'exposed to attack by misinterpretation'
64 *Application* i.e. of fiction to fact
69 *utter* in the sense 'pass false coin'
71 *raked up* raked over
77 *severe* F (Q grave) perhaps Q compositor's error influenced by 'grav'd, or Q corrected to avoid the chime
77 *patriots* fellow countrymen
77 *providing* foreseeing
79 *fools, and devils* figures in the old moralities and interludes
79 *antique* perhaps 'antic', grotesque
80 *exploded* clapped and hooted off the stage (*OED*)
82 *among* F (Q in)
83 *Sibi . . . odit* Horace, *Satires* II. i, 23, translated by Jonson: 'In satires, each man, though untouched, complains As he were hurt; and hates such biting strains' (*Poetaster* III. v, 41)

And men may justly impute such rages, if continued, to the writer, as his sports. The increase of which lust in liberty, 85 together with the present trade of the stage, in all their misc'line *interludes*, what learned or liberal soul doth not already abhor?—where nothing but the filth of the time is uttered, and that with such impropriety of phrase, such plenty of *solecisms*, such dearth of sense, so bold *prolepses*, so racked 90 *metaphors*, with brothelry, able to violate the ear of a pagan, and blasphemy to turn the blood of a Christian to water. I cannot but be serious in a cause of this nature, wherein my fame, and the reputations of divers honest and learned are the question; when a name, so full of authority, antiquity, and all great mark, 95 is (through their insolence) become the lowest scorn of the age: and those men subject to the petulancy of every vernaculous orator that were wont to be the care of Kings, and happiest Monarchs. This it is, that hath not only rapt me to present indignation, but made me studious heretofore; and by all my 100 actions to stand off, from them; which may most appear in this my latest work (which you, most learned *Arbitresses*, have seen, judged, and to my crown, approved) wherein I have laboured, for their instruction, and amendment, to reduce not only the ancient forms, but manners of the *scene*, the easiness, the pro- 105 priety, the innocence, and last the doctrine, which is the principal end of *poesie*, to inform men, in the best reason of living. And though my *catastrophe* may, in the strict rigour of *comic* law, meet with censure, as turning back to my promise; I desire the learned, and charitable critic to have so much faith 110 in me, to think it was done of industry. For, with what ease I could have varied it, nearer his scale (but that I fear to boast my own faculty) I could here insert. But my special aim being to put the snaffle in their mouths that cry out, we never punish vice in our interludes, &c., I took the more liberty; 115 though not without some lines of example, drawn even in the ancients themselves, the goings out of whose comedies are not

87 *misc'line* miscellane, jumbled (Latin *ludi miscelli*)
88 *filth* F (Q garbage)
95 *a name* i.e. 'poet', or specifically Horace, Jonson's voice in *The Poetaster* and his attributed name in Dekker's *Satiromastix*
97–98 *vernaculous* low-bred, scurrilous (Latin *vernaculus*, of home-born slaves)
99 *rapt me* carried me away
104 *reduce* restore (Latin *reduco*)
108 *catastrophe* dénouement
111 *of industry* deliberately (*of* ed. FQ off)
117 *goings out* endings

always joyful, but oft-times, the bawds, the servants, the rivals, yea, and the masters are mulcted: and fitly, it being the office of a *comic-Poet* to imitate justice, and instruct to life, as well as 120 purity of language, or stir up gentle affections. To which, I shall take the occasion elsewhere to speak. For the present (most reverenced Sisters) as I have cared to be thankful for your affections past, and here made the understanding acquainted with some ground of your favours; let me not despair 125 their continuance, to the maturing of some worthier fruits: wherein, if my *Muses* be true to me, I shall raise the despised head of *Poetry* again, and stripping her out of those rotten and base rags, wherewith the Times have adulterated her form, restore her to her primitive habit, feature and majesty, and 130 render her worthy to be embraced, and kissed, of all the great and master-spirits of our world. As for the vile, and slothful, who never affected an act worthy of celebration, or are so inward with their own vicious natures, as they worthily fear her; and think it a high point of policy, to keep her in contempt with 135 their declamatory, and windy invectives: she shall out of just rage incite her servants (who are *genus irritabile*) to spout ink in their faces, that shall eat, farther than their marrow, into their fames; and not Cinnamus the barber, with his art, shall be able to take out the brands, but they shall live, and be read, till the 140 wretches die, as things worst deserving of themselves in chief, and then of all mankind.

From my house in the Black-Friars
this 11. of February. 1607

121 *purity of language* governed by 'instruct to', but the construction falters in the next clause
122 *elsewhere* i.e. in his lost commentary on Horace's *Art of Poetry*
124 *the understanding* i.e. men of understanding
133 *affected* 'liked' or 'pretended to'
139 *Cinnamus* surgeon-barber celebrated by Martial (VI. lxiv, 26) for his skill in removing *stigmata*
141 *in chief* in the first place
143 *From . . . 1607* Q (F omits)
143 *Blackfriars* the centre of London's private theatres

THE PERSONS OF THE PLAY

VOLPONE, a Magnifico
MOSCA, his Parasite
VOLTORE, an Advocate
CORBACCIO, an old Gentleman

CORVINO, a Merchant
AVOCATORI, four Magistrates
NOTARIO, the Register
NANO, a Dwarf
CASTRONE, an Eunuch
GREGE [a crowd]

SIR POLITIC WOULD-BE, a Knight
PEREGRINE, a Gentleman-traveller
BONARIO, a young Gentleman
FINE MADAME WOULD-BE, the Knight's wife
CELIA, the Merchant's wife
COMMANDADORI, Officers
MERCATORI, three Merchants
ANDROGYNO, a Hermaphrodite
SERVITORE, a Servant
WOMEN

The Scene:
VENICE

VOLPONE 'an old fox, an old reinard, an old craftie, slie, subtle companion, sneaking lurking wily deceiver' (Florio, *A Worlde of Wordes* 1598)
MAGNIFICO magnate of Venice
MOSCA 'any kind of flye' (Florio); Beelzebub, the 'Prince of Devils', is in Hebrew 'the Lord of the flies'
VOLTORE 'a ravenous bird called a vultur, a geyre or grap. Also a greedie cormorant' (Florio)
CORBACCIO 'a filthie great raven' (Florio)
CORVINO crow; 'of a ravens nature or colour' (Florio 1611)
AVOCATORI state prosecutors
REGISTER clerk of the court
NANO Latin *nanus* a dwarf
PEREGRINE a hawk; a traveller
ANDROGYNO from Greek *andros* (man) and *gyne* (woman)
The Scene VENICE F (Q omits)

VOLPONE, OR THE FOXE

The Argument

V O L P O N E , childless, rich, feigns sick, despairs,
O ffers his state to hopes of several heirs,
L ies languishing; his Parasite receives
P resents of all, assures, deludes: then weaves
O ther cross-plots, which ope themselves, are told. 5
N ew tricks for safety are sought; they thrive; when, bold,
E ach tempts th'other again, and all are sold.

Prologue

Now, luck yet send us, and a little wit
  Will serve, to make our play hit;
According to the palates of the season,
  Here is rime, not empty of reason:
This we were bid to credit from our Poet, 5
  Whose true scope, if you would know it,
In all his poems, still, hath been this measure,
  To mix profit with your pleasure;
And not as some (whose throats their envy failing)
  Cry hoarsely, 'All he writes, is railing.' 10
And when his plays come forth, think they can flout them,
  With saying, 'He was a year about them.'
To these there needs no lie, but this his creature,
  Which was, two months since, no feature;
And, though he dares give them five lives to mend it, 15
  'Tis known, five weeks fully penned it;
From his own hand, without a coadjutor,
  Novice, journeyman, or tutor.
Yet, thus much I can give you, as a token
  Of his play's worth: no eggs are broken, 20

Argument the acrostic form is imitated from Plautus; *The Alchemist* also has one
2 *state* estate
1 *yet* F (Q God)
9 *as some* specifically Marston in *The Dutch Curtezan* (prologue)
12 *a year* 'you nasty tortoise, you and your itchy poetry break out like Christmas, but once a year' (*Satiromastix* V. ii, 217)
17 *coadjutor* Jonson worked with collaborators on *Eastward Ho*
18 *journeyman* qualified craftsman, more than novice but less than master

Nor quaking custards with fierce teeth affrighted,
Wherewith your rout are so delighted;
Nor hales he in a gull, old ends reciting,
To stop gaps in his loose writing,
With such a deal of monstrous, and forced action; 25
As might make Bet'lem a faction;
Nor made he his play, for jests, stol'n from each table,
But makes jests, to fit his fable.
And, so presents quick *comedy*, refined,
As best critics have designed; 30
The laws of time, place, persons he observeth,
From no needful rule he swerveth.
All gall, and copperas, from his ink, he draineth,
Only, a little salt remaineth,
Wherewith, he'll rub your cheeks, till, red with laughter, 35
They shall look fresh, a week after.

Act I, Scene i

[VOLPONE'S *house*]

[*Enter*] VOLPONE, MOSCA

VOLPONE
Good morning to the day; and, next, my gold!
Open the shrine, that I may see my saint.

[MOSCA *reveals the treasure*]

Hail the world's soul, and mine! More glad than is

21 *quaking custards* cowards, so taunted by Marston *Satire* II. iv; also perhaps custard-pie comedy, based on sport with huge custard at the Lord Mayor's feast
23 *gull* dupe, one who swallows anything (from gull = gorge)
23 *ends* tags
26 *make Bet'lem a faction* either 'make a party for the madhouse' or 'enlist the support of the madhouse'; Bet'lem, or Bedlam, was the asylum of St. Mary of Bethlehem
28 *fable* plot 29 *quick* lively
33 *gall, and copperas* oak galls and iron sulphate, used to make ink; rancour was attributed to the gall-bladder and copperas is bitter
34 *salt* is not used in ink, but iron sulphate was called 'salt of iron' and Jonson needs it to introduce the following joke out of Horace (*Satires* I. x, 3)
2 *shrine* Volpone is at his devotions and the treasure has the aspect of a holy reliquary
3 *world's soul* with a pun on 'sol', the sun; also perhaps the coin (see IV. v, 96–97)

The teeming earth to see the longed-for sun
Peep through the horns of the celestial Ram, 5
Am I, to view thy splendour, darkening his;
That, lying here, amongst my other hoards,
Show'st like a flame, by night; or like the day
Struck out of Chaos, when all darkness fled
Unto the centre. O, thou sun of Sol, 10
But brighter than thy father, let me kiss,
With adoration, thee, and every relic
Of sacred treasure, in this blessed room.
Well did wise Poets, by thy glorious name
Title that age, which they would have the best; 15
Thou being the best of things; and far transcending
All style of joy in children, parents, friends,
Or any other waking dream on earth.
Thy looks when they to Venus did ascribe,
They should have given her twenty thousand Cupids; 20
Such are thy beauties, and our loves! Dear *saint*,
Riches, the dumb god, that giv'st all men tongues;
That canst do nought, and yet mak'st men do all things;
The price of souls; even hell, with thee to boot,
Is made worth heaven! Thou art virtue, fame, 25
Honour, and all things else! Who can get thee,
He shall be noble, valiant, honest, wise—

MOSCA

And what he will, sir. Riches are in fortune
A greater good, than wisdom is in nature.

VOLPONE

True, my beloved Mosca. Yet, I glory 30
More in the cunning purchase of my wealth,
Than in the glad possession; since I gain
No common way: I use no trade, no venture;

5 *celestial Ram* the sun enters Aries at the spring equinox
8–9 *day . . . Chaos* the first day of creation (*Genesis* I.2–4)
10 *sun of Sol* alchemy held gold to be the offspring of the sun
12 *relic* i.e. the kind found in a shrine
15 *that age* the Golden Age (described by Ovid, *Met.* I.89–112)
19 *Venus . . . ascribe* following Homeric tradition the Latin poets often called Venus 'golden' (*aurea*)
22 *the dumb god* 'silence is golden'
25–27 *Thou art . . . wise* compare Horace, *Satires* II. iii, 94
28–29 *Riches . . . nature* 'Better to be endowed by chance with riches than by nature with wisdom'
31 *purchase* procurance

I wound no earth with ploughshares; fat no beasts
To feed the shambles; have no mills for iron, 35
Oil, corn, or men, to grind 'em into poulder;
I blow no subtle glass; expose no ships
To threat'nings of the furrow-faced sea;
I turn no moneys, in the public bank;
Nor usure private—

MOSCA No, sir, nor devour 40
Soft prodigals. You shall ha' some will swallow
A melting heir, as glibly as your Dutch
Will pills of butter, and ne'er purge for't
Tear forth the fathers of poor families
Out of their beds, and coffin them alive 45
In some kind, clasping prison, where their bones
May be forth-coming, when the flesh is rotten:
But your sweet nature doth abhor these courses;
You loathe, the widow's, or the orphan's tears
Should wash your pavements; or their piteous cries 50
Ring in your roofs; and beat the air, for vengeance—

VOLPONE
Right, Mosca, I do loathe it.

MOSCA And besides, sir,
You are not like the thresher, that doth stand
With a huge flail, watching a heap of corn,
And, hungry, dares not taste the smallest grain, 55
But feeds on mallows, and such bitter herbs;
Not like the merchant, who hath filled his vaults
With Romagnia, and rich Candian wines,
Yet drinks the lees of Lombard's vinegar;
You will not lie in straw, whilst moths, and worms 60
Feed on your sumptuous hangings, and soft beds.
You know the use of riches, and dare give, now,

35 *shambles* slaughterhouse
36 *grind 'em* i.e. exploit the men; compare *New Inn* II. v, 119 'His mills, to grind his servants into powder'
37 *subtle* tenuous, delicate; Venice was famed for its glass
39 *turn* exchange
40 *usure* exchange at high interest
40 *private* privately
42–43 *Dutch . . . butter* a notorious Dutch weakness; compare *Every Man In* III. iv, 42
53 *the thresher* from Horace, *Satires* II. iii, 111
58 *Romagnia* Rumney, a sweet Greek wine
58 *Candian wines* Malmsey from Candy (Crete)

From that bright heap, to me, your poor observer,
Or to your dwarf, or your hermaphrodite,
Your eunuch, or what other household trifle 65
Your pleasure allows maintenance—

VOLPONE Hold thee, Mosca,

[*Gives him money*]

Take, of my hand; thou strik'st on truth, in all:
And they are envious term thee parasite.
Call forth my dwarf, my eunuch, and my fool,
And let 'em make me sport. What should I do, 70
But cocker up my *genius*, and live free
To all delights, my fortune calls me to?
I have no wife, no parent, child, ally,
To give my substance to; but whom I make
Must be my heir: and this makes men observe me. 75
This draws new clients, daily, to my house,
Women, and men, of every sex and age,
That bring me presents, send me plate, coin, jewels,
With hope, that when I die (which they expect
Each greedy minute) it shall then return, 80
Tenfold, upon them; whilst some, covetous
Above the rest, seek to engross me, whole,
And counter-work, the one, unto the other,
Contend in gifts, as they would seem, in love:
All which I suffer, playing with their hopes, 85
And am content to coin 'em into profit,
And look upon their kindness, and take more,
And look on that; still bearing them in hand,
Letting the cherry knock against their lips,
And, draw it, by their mouths, and back again. How now! 90

66 *Hold thee* keep for yourself
71 *cocker up* pamper, indulge (Latin *indulgere genio*)
75 *observe* 'treat with ceremonious respect or reverence' (*OED*)
76 *clients* followers who wait upon the patronage of Volpone the Magnifico (ironic)
88 *still* continually
88 *bearing . . . hand* leading them on
89 *cherry* in the game of chop-cherry the player tried to bite a dangling cherry

Act I, Scene ii

[*Enter* MOSCA, *with* NANO, ANDROGYNO, *and* CASTRONE]
[*An entertainment follows*]

NANO

Now, room for fresh gamesters, who do will you to know,
They do bring you neither play, nor University show;
And therefore do intreat you, that whatsoever they rehearse,
May not fare a whit the worse, for the false pace of the verse.
If you wonder at this, you will wonder more, ere we pass, 5
For know [*Pointing to* ANDROGYNO], here is enclosed the Soul of Pythagoras,
That juggler divine, as hereafter shall follow;
Which soul, fast and loose, sir, came first from Apollo,
And was breathed into Aethalides, Mercurius his son,
Where it had the gift to remember all that ever was done. 10
From thence it fled forth, and made quick transmigration
To goldy-locked Euphorbus, who was killed, in good fashion,
At the siege of old Troy, by the cuckold of Sparta.
Hermotimus was next (I find it in my charta)
To whom it did pass, where no sooner it was missing, 15
But with one Pyrrhus, of Delos, it learned to go a fishing:

3 *rehearse* recite

4 *false pace* exemplified by Nano as he speaks; the old-fashioned loose four-stress rhythm, with forced rhymes, falsifies the natural sense

6 *Pythagoras* for other glimpses of 'metempsychosis' or transmigration of the soul, see *Twelfth Night* IV. ii, 57–64, and *Dr. Faustus* V. ii, 172–174. The history of his own soul is told by Lucian, 'Dialogue of the Cobbler and the Cock' and by Diogenes Laertius (see Introduction, p. xxi)

8 *fast and loose* 'slippery, hard to catch', from a betting game in which one player guessed whether or not a dagger was held fast in a belt intricately folded by the other

9 *Aethalides* herald to the Argonauts and heir to an omniscient memory

12 *Euphorbus* the Trojan who first wounded Patroclus (*Iliad* 17)

13 *cuckold of Sparta* Menelaus

14 *Hermotimus* a Greek philosopher

14 *charta* paper, perhaps Lucian's dialogue

16 *Pyrrhus, of Delos* a philosopher; the name and the allusion to fishing are supplied by Diogenes Laertius without explanation

And thence did it enter the Sophist of Greece.
From Pythagore, she went into a beautiful piece,
Hight Aspasia, the meretrix; and the next toss of her
Was, again, of a whore, she became a philosopher, 20
Crates the Cynic: as itself does relate it.
Since, kings, knights, and beggars, knaves, lords and fools gat it,
Besides, ox, and ass, camel, mule, goat, and brock,
In all which it hath spoke, as in the cobbler's cock.
But I come not here, to discourse of that matter, 25
Or his one, two, or three, or his great oath, 'By Quater!'
His musics, his trigon, his golden thigh,
Or his telling how elements shift; but I
Would ask, how of late, thou hast suffered translation,
And shifted thy coat, in these days of reformation? 30

ANDROGYNO
Like one of the reformèd, a fool, as you see,
Counting all old doctrine heresy.

NANO
But not on thine own forbid meats hast thou ventured?

ANDROGYNO
On fish, when first, a Carthusian I entered.

NANO
Why, then thy dogmatical silence hath left thee? 35

ANDROGYNO
Of that an obstreperous lawyer bereft me.

17 *Sophist of Greece* Pythagoras is so styled by Lucian
19 *Hight* (Old English) named, called *Aspasia* mistress of Pericles
19 *meretrix* courtesan 21 *Crates* a pupil of Diogenes
21 *itself* either the cock in Lucian, or Androgyno
24 *cobbler's cock* the cock tells the story in Lucian
26 *Quater* the Pythagorean trigon or triangle of four, symbol of cosmic and moral harmony: .:.:.
27 *musics* Pythagorean theory related the spacing of the cosmic spheres to the laws of harmony
27 *golden thigh* attributed to Pythagoras by his followers
30 *reformation* the Protestant reformation; Jonson was still a Catholic in 1606
31 *reformèd* evidently the Puritans
33 *forbid meats* forbidden foods; Pythagoreans were forbidden fish and beans
34 *Carthusian* an order strict in its diet but allowing fish
35 *dogmatical silence* Pythagoreans were enjoined to a five-year silence, which might have been maintained among the Carthusians
36 *obstreperous* vociferous

NANO
O wonderful change! when Sir Lawyer forsook thee,
For Pythagore's sake, what body then took thee?
ANDROGYNO
A good dull moyle.
NANO And how! by that means,
Thou wert brought to allow of the eating of beans? 40
ANDROGYNO
Yes.
NANO But, from the moyle, into whom did'st thou pass?
ANDROGYNO
Into a very strange beast, by some writers called an ass;
By others, a precise, pure, illuminate brother,
Of those devour flesh, and sometimes one another;
And will drop forth a libel, or a sanctified lie, 45
Betwixt every spoonful of a nativity-pie.
NANO
Now quit thee, for heaven, of that profane nation;
And gently, report thy next transmigration.
ANDROGYNO
To the same that I am.
NANO A creature of delight?
And, what is more than a fool, an hermaphrodite? 50
Now pray thee, sweet soul, in all thy variation,
Which body would'st thou choose, to take up thy station?
ANDROGYNO
Troth, this I am in, even here would I tarry.
NANO
'Cause here, the delight of each sex thou canst vary?
ANDROGYNO
Alas, those pleasures be stale, and forsaken; 55
No, 'tis your fool, wherewith I am so taken;
The only one creature, that I can call blessed,
For all other forms I have proved most distressed.
NANO
Spoke true, as thou wert in Pythagoras still.
This learned opinion we celebrate will, 60
Fellow eunuch, as behoves us, with all our wit and art,

39 *moyle* mule
43 *precise* 'strict in religious observance, puritanical' (*OED*)
43 *illuminate* visionary
46 *nativity-pie* Christmas pie, evading the word 'mass', see *The Alchemist* III. ii, 43

To dignify that whereof our selves are so great, and special a part.

VOLPONE
Now very, very pretty! Mosca, this
Was thy invention?

MOSCA If it please my patron,
Not else.

VOLPONE It doth, good Mosca.

MOSCA Then it was, sir. 65

Song

Fools, they are the only nation
Worth men's envy, or admiration;
Free from care, or sorrow-taking,
Selves, and others merry making: 70
All they speak, or do, is sterling.
Your Fool, he is your great man's dearling,
And your ladies' sport, and pleasure;
Tongue, and bable are his treasure.
E'en his face begetteth laughter, 75
And he speaks truth, free from slaughter;
He's the grace of every feast,
And, sometimes, the chiefest guest;
Hath his trencher, and his stool,
When wit waits upon the fool. 80
O, who would not be
He, he, he? *One knocks without*

VOLPONE
Who's that? Away! [*Exeunt* NANO, CASTRONE]
Look Mosca!

MOSCA Fool, begone!
[*Exit* ANDROGYNO]

'Tis Signior Voltore, the advocate;
I know him, by his knock.

62 *that* i.e. folly
66 *Song* it might be sung by the grotesques, by Mosca alone, or by all
67 *nation* sect
71 *sterling* capable of standing every test
74 *bable* the fool's bauble or sceptre; slang for phallus
76 *free from slaughter* without being called to account; Marston mocked Jonson for rhyming laughter/slaughter (*The Fawn* IV. i), but compare the fool's song in *Lear* I. iv, 340; fool's licence?
80 *wit . . . fool* the fool dines off his host; wit waits upon the fool's words

VOLPONE Fetch me my gown, 85
My furs, and night caps; say, my couch is changing:
And let him entertain himself, awhile,
Without i' th' gallery. Now, now, my clients
Begin their visitation! vulture, kite,
Raven, and gor-crow, all my birds of prey, 90
That think me turning carcass, now they come.
I am not for 'em yet. How now? the news? [*Enter* MOSCA]

MOSCA
A piece of plate, sir.

VOLPONE Of what bigness?

MOSCA Huge,
Massy, and antique, with your name inscribed,
And arms engraven.

VOLPONE Good! and not a fox 95
Stretched on the earth, with fine delusive sleights,
Mocking a gaping crow? ha, Mosca?

MOSCA Sharp, sir.

VOLPONE
Give me my furs. Why dost thou laugh so, man?

MOSCA
I cannot choose, sir, when I apprehend
What thoughts he has, without, now, as he walks: 100
That this might be the last gift he should give;
That this would fetch you; if you died today,
And gave him all, what he should be tomorrow;
What large return would come of all his ventures;
How he should worshipped be, and reverenced; 105
Ride, with his furs, and foot-cloths; waited on
By herds of fools, and clients; have clear way
Made for his moyle, as lettered as himself;
Be called the great, and learned advocate:
And then concludes, there's nought impossible. 110

VOLPONE
Yes, to be learned, Mosca.

MOSCA O, no: rich

86 *furs* worn by the sick for warmth
90 *gor-crow* carrion crow
95–97 *fox . . . crow* for a similar application of the fable of the crow, dropping its cheese as it sings for the adulatory fox, see Horace, *Satires* II. v, 55
104 *ventures* enterprising investments; compare I. i, 33
106 *foot-cloths* pageant drapery for a horse

Implies it. Hood an ass with reverend purple,
So you can hide his two ambitious ears,
And he shall pass for a cathedral doctor.

VOLPONE
My caps, my caps, good Mosca. Fetch him in. 115

MOSCA
Stay, sir, your ointment for your eyes.

VOLPONE
That's true;
Dispatch, dispatch: I long to have possession
Of my new present.

MOSCA
That, and thousands more,
I hope to see you lord of.

VOLPONE
Thanks, kind Mosca.

MOSCA
And that, when I am lost in blended dust, 120
And hundred such as I am, in succession—

VOLPONE
Nay, that were too much, Mosca.

MOSCA
You shall live,
Still, to delude these harpies.

VOLPONE
Loving Mosca!

[*Looking into a glass*]

112 *reverend purple* crimson robes of a Doctor of Divinity
115 *caps* probably ear-caps, prompted by line 113, at this point, perhaps, Volpone gets into bed
116 *ointment* to make his eyes sticky and rheumy

112-114 *Hood . . . doctor* one of the recurrent jokes in Erasmus's *Praise of Folly* (see Fig. 1, p. vi). Folly tells how others try to hide their own foolishness: 'So that not so muche as they can dissemble me, who take upon theim most semblant of wysedome, and walke lyke Asses in Lyons skinnes. That although they counterfeite what they can, yet on some syde their long eares pearyng foorth, dooe discover them to come of Midas progenie. . . . So that some be of such a vaingloriousness, as whan they can least skyll thereof, yet will they flire, and nodde the head at it, and (as the Asse doeth) wagge theyr eares, to make others beleve that they are depely seen therin.' (Chaloner's translation, 1549 (1965), pp. 10–11). Erasmus's Latin may have suggested the pun on 'ambitious' that Chaloner's 'vaingloriousness' misses: 'Quod si qui paulo sunt ambitiosiores, arrideant tamen & applaudant, atque asini exemplo. . . .' (*Opera* 1703 (1962), IV, 409B). Holbein makes much of the joke, featuring the ass's ears in three further illustrations (*Opera* IV, 442C, 450B, 464B); in the last one the satire is specifically upon Doctors of Divinity.

'Tis well! My pillow now, and let him enter

[*Exit* MOSCA]

Now, my feigned cough, my phthisic, and my gout, 125
My apoplexy, palsie, and catarrhs,
Help, with your forced functions, this my posture,
Wherein, this three year, I have milked their hopes.
He comes, I hear him—uh! uh! uh! uh! O—

Act I, Scene iii

[*Enter* MOSCA, *with* VOLTORE *bearing plate.* VOLPONE *in bed*]

MOSCA
You still are what you were, sir. Only you,
Of all the rest, are he, commands his love:
And you do wisely, to preserve it, thus,
With early visitation, and kind notes
Of your good meaning to him, which, I know, 5
Cannot but come most grateful. Patron, sir!
Here's Signior Voltore is come—

VOLPONE What say you?

MOSCA
Sir, Signior Voltore is come, this morning,
To visit you.

VOLPONE I thank him.

125–127 *Now . . . posture* a sacrilegious invocation in the epic manner to the powers of feigned disease
125 *phthisic* consumption or asthma
127 *posture* pose, imposture
4 *notes* signs
5 *good meaning* well-wishing

Act I, Scene iii. 'This and the following scenes are really a Roman *salutio* i.e. the morning visit of clients to their patron so often referred to and described by the satirists.' (Rea)

In Lucian's Dialogues of the Dead 19 (9) Polystratus, who has at last died at ninety-eight, tells how his admirers flocked to his door at dawn, bearing him gifts from all corners of the earth: 'I would keep saying in public that I had left each of them my heir, and each would believe me, and show himself more assiduous than ever in his flattery.' (*Loeb* edition (1961), VII, p. 99). See also p. 158 below.

MOSCA And hath brought
A piece of antique plate, bought of St. Mark, 10
With which he here presents you.

VOLPONE He is welcome.
Pray him, to come more often.

MOSCA Yes.

VOLTORE What says he?

MOSCA
He thanks you, and desires you to see him often.

VOLPONE
Mosca!

MOSCA My patron?

VOLPONE Bring him near, where is he?
I long to feel his hand.

MOSCA [*Guiding Volpone's hand*] The plate is here, sir. 15

VOLTORE
How fare you, sir?

VOLPONE I thank you, Signior Voltore.
Where is the plate? Mine eyes are bad.

VOLTORE [*Putting it into his hand*] I'm sorry
To see you still thus weak.

MOSCA [*Aside*] That he is not weaker.

VOLPONE
You are too munificent.

VOLTORE No, sir, would to heaven,
I could as well give health to you, as that plate. 20

VOLPONE
You give, sir, what you can. I thank you. Your love
Hath taste in this, and shall not be unanswered.
I pray you see me often.

VOLTORE Yes, I shall, sir.

VOLPONE
Be not far from me.

MOSCA (*To Voltore*) Do you observe that, sir?

VOLPONE
Hearken unto me, still: it will concern you. 25

MOSCA
You are a happy man, sir, know your good.

VOLPONE
I cannot now last long—

10 *of St. Mark* in St. Mark's Square, celebrated for its goldsmiths' shops
22 *Hath taste in* can be felt in

MOSCA You are his heir, sir.

VOLTORE
Am I?

VOLPONE I feel me going, uh! uh! uh! uh!
I am sailing to my port, uh! uh! uh! uh!
And I am glad, I am so near my haven. 30

MOSCA
Alas, kind gentleman; well, we must all go—

VOLTORE
But, Mosca—

MOSCA Age will conquer.

VOLTORE Pray thee hear me.
Am I inscribed his heir, for certain?

MOSCA Are you?
I do beseech you, sir, you will vouchsafe
To write me, i' your family. All my hopes 35
Depend upon your worship. I am lost,
Except the rising sun do shine on me.

VOLTORE
It shall both shine, and warm thee, Mosca.

MOSCA Sir,
I am a man that have not done your love
All the worst offices: here I wear your keys, 40
See all your coffers and your caskets locked,
Keep the poor inventory of your jewels,
Your plate, and monies; am your steward, sir,
Husband your goods here.

VOLTORE But am I sole heir?

MOSCA
Without a partner, sir, confirmed this morning; 45
The wax is warm yet, and the ink scarce dry
Upon the parchment.

VOLTORE Happy, happy, me!
By what good chance, sweet Mosca?

MOSCA Your desert, sir;
I know no second cause.

VOLTORE Thy modesty
Is loath to know it; well, we shall requite it. 50

35 *write . . . family* names of servants were entered in a 'Household Book'
38–44 Possibly suggested by Horace, *Satires* II. v, 47–49
40 *your keys* i.e. Voltore's because Volpone's
50 *know it* acknowledge it

MOSCA

He ever liked your course, sir, that first took him.
I, oft, have heard him say, how he admired
Men of your large profession, that could speak
To every cause, and things mere contraries,
Till they were hoarse again, yet all be law; 55
That, with most quick agility, could turn,
And re-turn; make knots, and undo them;
Give forkèd counsel; take provoking gold
On either hand, and put it up: these men,
He knew, would thrive, with their humility. 60
And, for his part, he thought, he should be bless'd
To have his heir of such a suffering spirit,
So wise, so grave, of so perplexed a tongue,
And loud withall, that would not wag, nor scarce
Lie still, without a fee; when every word 65
Your worship but lets fall, is a chequeen!

Another knocks

Who's that? one knocks; I would not have you seen, sir.
And yet—pretend you came, and went in haste;
I'll fashion an excuse. And, gentle sir,
When you do come to swim, in golden lard, 70
Up to the arms, in honey, that your chin
Is born up stiff, with fatness of the flood,
Think on your vassal; but remember me:
I ha' not been your worst of clients.

VOLTORE

Mosca—

MOSCA

When will you have your inventory brought, sir? 75
Or see a copy of the will? [*Knocking again*] Anon!
I'll bring 'em to you, sir. Away, be gone
Put business in your face. [*Exit* VOLTORE]

VOLPONE

Excellent, Mosca!
Come hither, let me kiss thee.

51 *course* way of doing things 51 *took* captivated
51–55 Suggested by Horace, *Satires* II. v, 33–34, and Cornelius Agrippa, *De Incertitudine* ch. 93
53 *large* liberal, expansive and eloquent 58 *forkèd* equivocal
58 *provoking gold* court fees (provoke, 'to call to a judge or court to take up one's cause' *OED*)
59 *either hand* for either party
59 *put it up* either 'deposit it' or (Mosca's real meaning) 'pocket it'
63 *perplexed* involved, puzzling
66 *chequeen* (F cecchine) Venetian gold coin, sequin

MOSCA Keep you still, sir.
Here is Corbaccio.
VOLPONE Set the plate away. 80
The vulture's gone, and the old raven's come.

Act I, Scene iv

MOSCA
Betake you to your silence, and your sleep.
[*Sets plate aside*] Stand there, and multiply. Now we shall see
A wretch who is indeed more impotent
Than this can feign to be; yet hopes to hop
Over his grave. [*Enter* CORBACCIO] Signior Corbaccio! 5
You're very welcome, sir.
CORBACCIO How does your patron?
MOSCA
Troth, as he did, sir, no amends.
CORBACCIO What? mends he?
MOSCA
No, sir: he is rather worse.
CORBACCIO That's well. Where is he?
MOSCA
Upon his couch, sir, newly fall'n asleep.
CORBACCIO
Does he sleep well?
MOSCA No wink, sir, all this night, 10
Nor yesterday, but slumbers.
CORBACCIO Good! He should take
Some counsel of physicians; I have brought him
An opiate here, from mine own doctor—
MOSCA
He will not hear of drugs.
CORBACCIO Why? I myself
Stood by, while 't was made; saw all th' ingredients; 15
And know, it cannot but most gently work.
My life for his, 'tis but to make him sleep.
VOLPONE [*Aside*]
Ay, his last sleep, if he would take it.
MOSCA Sir,
He has no faith in physic.
CORBACCIO Say you, say you?

11 *slumbers* dozes

MOSCA
He has no faith in physic: he does think 20
Most of your doctors are the greater danger,
And worse disease t'escape. I often have
Heard him protest, that your physician
Should never be his heir.
CORBACCIO Not I his heir?
MOSCA
Not your physician, sir.
CORBACCIO O, no, no, no, 25
I do not mean it.
MOSCA No, sir, nor their fees
He cannot brook: he says, they flay a man
Before they kill him.
CORBACCIO Right, I do conceive you.
MOSCA
And then, they do it by experiment;
For which the law not only doth absolve 'em, 30
But gives them great reward: and he is loath
To hire his death, so.
CORBACCIO It is true, they kill,
With as much licence, as a judge.
MOSCA Nay, more;
For he but kills, sir, where the law condemns,
And these can kill him, too.
CORBACCIO Ay, or me: 35
Or any man. How does his apoplex?
Is that strong on him still?
MOSCA Most violent.
His speech is broken, and his eyes are set,
His face drawn longer than 't was wont—
CORBACCIO How? How?
Stronger than he was wont?
MOSCA No, sir: his face 40
Drawn longer, than 't was wont.
CORBACCIO O, good.
MOSCA His mouth

21, 25 *your* i.e. doctors and physicians in general; the satire upon the medical profession owes much to Cornelius Agrippa, *De Vanitate* (see Introduction, p. xxi)
27 *flay* strip off skin
28 *conceive* understand
29 *experiment* trial, upon the patient
36 *apoplex* apoplexy; Hippocrates held the 'strong apoplex' incurable

Is ever gaping, and his eyelids hang.

CORBACCIO Good.

MOSCA

A freezing numbness stiffens all his joints,
And makes the colour of his flesh like lead.

CORBACCIO 'Tis good.

MOSCA

His pulse beats slow, and dull.

CORBACCIO Good symptoms, still. 45

MOSCA

And, from his brain—

CORBACCIO Ha? How? Not from his brain?

MOSCA

Yes, sir, and from his brain—

CORBACCIO I conceive you, good.

MOSCA

Flows a cold sweat, with a continual rheum,
Forth the resolvèd corners of his eyes.

CORBACCIO

Is't possible? Yet I am better, ha! 50
How does he, with the swimming of his head?

MOSCA

O, sir, 'tis past the *scotomy*; he, now,
Hath lost his feeling, and hath left to snort;
You hardly can perceive him, that he breathes.

CORBACCIO

Excellent, excellent, sure I shall outlast him: 55
This makes me young again, a score of years.

MOSCA

I was a-coming for you, sir.

CORBACCIO Has he made his will?
What has he given me?

MOSCA No, sir.

CORBACCIO Nothing? ha?

MOSCA

He has not made his will, sir.

CORBACCIO Oh, oh, oh.
What then did Voltore, the lawyer, here? 60

46 *from his brain* drainage of brain fluid was believed the last stage of strong apoplexy, and Corbaccio eagerly recognises its significance
49 *resolvèd* slackened
52 *scotomy* 'dizziness accompanied by dimness of sight' (*OED*)
53 *left* ceased
60 *What then did* F (Q But what did)

MOSCA
He smelt a carcass, sir, when he but heard
My master was about his testament;
As I did urge him to it, for your good—

CORBACCIO
He came unto him, did he? I thought so.

MOSCA
Yes, and presented him this piece of plate. 65

CORBACCIO
To be his heir?

MOSCA I do not know, sir.

CORBACCIO True,
I know it too.

MOSCA By your own scale, sir.

CORBACCIO Well,
I shall prevent him, yet. See, Mosca, look,
Here, I have brought a bag of bright chequeens,
Will quite weigh down his plate.

MOSCA Yea, marry, sir! 70
This is true physic, this your sacred medicine,
No talk of *opiates*, to this great *elixir*.

CORBACCIO
'Tis *aurum palpabile*, if not *potabile*.

MOSCA
It shall be ministered to him in his bowl?

CORBACCIO
Ay, do, do, do.

MOSCA Most blessed cordial! 75
This will recover him.

CORBACCIO Yes, do, do, do.

MOSCA
I think, it were not best, sir.

CORBACCIO What?

MOSCA To recover him.

67 *By . . . scale* either 'by your own estimation, without my help' or 'judging by your own case'
68 *prevent* keep in front of
70 *weigh down* outweigh; perhaps suggested by Mosca's 'scale'
72 *elixir* alchemical essence fabled to make life eternal; analogous to the 'stone' thought to eternalise base metal into gold
73 *aurum . . . potabile* 'palpable, if not drinkable, gold'
73 *aurum potabile* was held a sovereign remedy for all diseases
75 *cordial* a medicine to invigorate the heart, e.g. potable gold

CORBACCIO
O, no, no, no; by no means.
MOSCA Why, sir, this
Will work some strange effect, if he but feel it.
CORBACCIO
'Tis true, therefore forbear, I'll take my venture: 80
Give me 't again.
MOSCA At no hand, pardon me;
You shall not do yourself that wrong, sir. I
Will so advise you, you shall have it all.
CORBACCIO
How?
MOSCA All, sir, 'tis your right, your own; no man
Can claim a part: 'tis yours, without a rival, 85
Decreed by destiny.
CORBACCIO How? how, good Mosca?
MOSCA
I'll tell you, sir. This fit he shall recover—
CORBACCIO
I do conceive you.
MOSCA And, on first advantage
Of his gained sense, will I re-importune him
Unto the making of his testament; 90
And show him this.
CORBACCIO Good, good.
MOSCA 'Tis better yet,
If you will hear, sir.
CORBACCIO Yes, with all my heart.
MOSCA
Now, would I counsel you, make home with speed;
There, frame a will: whereto you shall inscribe
My master your sole heir.
CORBACCIO And disinherit 95
My son?
MOSCA O, sir, the better: for that colour
Shall make it much more taking.
CORBACCIO O, but colour?

80 *venture* i.e. the bag of gold
88 *advantage* opportunity
89 *gained* regained
94 *frame* devise
94 *whereto* to the end that
96 *colour* semblance
97 *taking* attractive

MOSCA
This will, sir, you shall send it unto me.
Now, when I come to enforce, as I will do,
Your cares, your watchings, and your many prayers, 100
Your more than many gifts, your this day's present,
And, last, produce your will; where, without thought,
Or least regard, unto your proper issue,
A son so brave, and highly meriting,
The stream of your diverted love hath thrown you 105
Upon my master, and made him your heir:
He cannot be so stupid, or stone dead,
But, out of conscience, and mere gratitude—

CORBACCIO
He must pronounce me, his?

MOSCA
'Tis true.

CORBACCIO
This plot
Did I think on before.

MOSCA
I do believe it. 110

CORBACCIO
Do you not believe it?

MOSCA
Yes, sir.

CORBACCIO
Mine own project.

MOSCA
Which when he hath done, sir—

CORBACCIO
Published me his heir?

MOSCA
And you so certain to survive him—

CORBACCIO
Ay.

MOSCA
Being so lusty a man—

CORBACCIO
'Tis true.

MOSCA
Yes, sir.

CORBACCIO
I thought on that too. See, how he should be 115
The very organ, to express my thoughts!

MOSCA
You have not only done yourself a good—

CORBACCIO
But multiplied it on my son?

MOSCA
'Tis right, sir.

99 *enforce* urge
103 *proper issue* own true offspring
115 *See . . . be* 'See, if he isn't . . .'
116 *organ* medium, instrument

CORBACCIO
Still, my invention.
MOSCA 'Las, sir, heaven knows,
It hath been all my study, all my care, 120
(I e'en grow grey withal) how to work things—
CORBACCIO
I do conceive, sweet Mosca.
MOSCA You are he,
For whom I labour, here.
CORBACCIO Ay, do, do, do:
I'll straight about it. [*Begins to go*]
MOSCA [*Aside*] Rook go with you, raven.
CORBACCIO
I know thee honest.
MOSCA You do lie, sir.
CORBACCIO And— 125
MOSCA
Your knowledge is no better than your ears, sir.
CORBACCIO
I do not doubt, to be a father to thee.
MOSCA
Nor I, to gull my brother of his blessing.
CORBACCIO
I may ha' my youth restored to me, why not?
MOSCA
Your worship is a precious ass—
CORBACCIO What say'st thou? 130
MOSCA
I do desire your worship, to make haste, sir.
CORBACCIO
'Tis done, 'tis done, I go. [*Exit* CORBACCIO]
VOLPONE [*Leaping up*] O I shall burst;
Let out my sides, let out my sides—
MOSCA Contain
Your flux of laughter, sir. You know this hope
Is such a bait, it covers any hook. 135
VOLPONE
O, but thy working, and thy placing it!

119 *Still, my invention* echoes 'Mine own project'
119 *'Las* Alas 124 *straight* immediately
124 *Rook go with you* 'may you be rooked'
126 *Your . . . ears* both a taunt and a strict truth
128 *my brother* i.e. Corbaccio's son, with a glance at Jacob's cheating of Esau (*Genesis* 27) 134 *flux* flow, morbid discharge

I cannot hold; good rascal, let me kiss thee:
I never knew thee, in so rare a humour.

MOSCA
Alas, sir, I but do, as I am taught;
Follow your grave instructions; give 'em words; 140
Pour oil into their ears; and send them hence.

VOLPONE
'Tis true, 'tis true. What a rare punishment
Is avarice, to itself!

MOSCA
Ay, with our help, sir.

VOLPONE
So many cares, so many maladies,
So many fears attending on old age, 145
Yea, death so often called on, as no wish
Can be more frequent with 'em, their limbs faint,
Their senses dull, their seeing, hearing, going,
All dead before them; yea, their very teeth,
Their instruments of eating, failing them: 150
Yet this is reckoned life! Nay, here was one,
Is now gone home, that wishes to live longer!
Feels not his gout, nor palsy, feigns himself
Younger by scores of years, flatters his age,
With confident belying it, hopes he may 155
With charms, like Aeson, have his youth restored:
And with these thoughts so battens, as if fate
Would be as easily cheated on, as he,
And all turns air! *Another knocks* Who's that, there, now?
a third?

MOSCA
Close, to your couch again; I hear his voice. 160
It is Corvino, our spruce merchant.

VOLPONE [*Lying down*] Dead.

MOSCA
Another bout, sir, with your eyes. Who's there?

138 *rare a humour* fine and inventive mood
140 *give 'em words* deceive (proverbial)
141 *Pour . . . ears* deceive with fulsome words (proverbial)
144–151 *So many . . . life* derived largely from Pliny *Nat. Hist.* 7 167–168 (see Introduction p. xx); compare *Measure for Measure* III. i, 5–40
148 *going* ability to walk
156 *Aeson* Jason's father, whose youth was restored by Medea's magic
157 *battens* grows fat
162 *Another bout* Mosca applies more ointment

Act I, Scene v

[*Enter* CORVINO]

MOSCA
Signior Corvino! come most wished for! O,
How happy were you, if you knew it, now!

CORVINO
Why? what? wherein?

MOSCA
The tardy hour is come, sir.

CORVINO
He is not dead?

MOSCA
Not dead, sir, but as good;
He knows no man.

CORVINO
How shall I do, then?

MOSCA
Why, sir? 5

CORVINO
I have brought him, here, a pearl.

MOSCA
Perhaps he has
So much remembrance left, as to know you, sir;
He still calls on you, nothing but your name
Is in his mouth; is your pearl orient, sir?

CORVINO
Venice was never owner of the like. 10

VOLPONE [*Faintly*]
Signior Corvino.

MOSCA
Hark.

VOLPONE
Signior Corvino.

MOSCA
He calls you, step and give it him. He's here, sir.
And he has brought you a rich pearl.

CORVINO
How do you, sir?
Tell him it doubles the twelfth carat.

MOSCA
Sir,
He cannot understand, his hearing's gone; 15
And yet it comforts him, to see you—

CORVINO
Say,
I have a diamant for him, too.

MOSCA
Best show't, sir,
Put it into his hand; 'tis only there

9 *orient* eastern pearls were of superior value and brilliancy
14 *carat* measure of weight of precious stones (then 3⅓ grains)
17 *diamant* Jonson anachronistically preferred this Middle English form

He apprehends: he has his feeling, yet.
[VOLPONE *seizes the pearl*]
See, how he grasps it!

CORVINO 'Las, good gentleman! 20
How pitiful the sight is!

MOSCA Tut, forget, sir.
The weeping of an heir should still be laughter,
Under a visor.

CORVINO Why? am I his heir?

MOSCA
Sir, I am sworn, I may not show the will,
Till he be dead: but, here has been Corbaccio, 25
Here has been Voltore, here were others too,
I cannot number 'em, they were so many,
All gaping here for legacies, but I,
Taking the vantage of his naming you,
'Signior Corvino, Signior Corvino', took 30
Paper, and pen, and ink, and there I asked him,
Whom he would have his heir? 'Corvino'. Who
Should be executor? 'Corvino'. And
To any question he was silent to,
I still interpreted the nods he made, 35
Through weakness, for consent; and sent home th'others,
Nothing bequeathed them, but to cry, and curse.

They embrace

CORVINO
O, my dear Mosca. Does he not perceive us?

MOSCA
No more than a blind harper. He knows no man,
No face of friend, nor name of any servant, 40
Who 'twas that fed him last, or gave him drink:
Not those, he hath begotten, or brought up
Can he remember.

CORVINO Has he children?

MOSCA Bastards,
Some dozen, or more, that he begot on beggars,
Gipsies, and Jews, and black-moors, when he was drunk. 45
Knew you not that, sir? 'Tis the common fable,

22–23 *The weeping . . . visor* echoing Horace, *Satires* II. v, 103
23 *visor* a mask
30 *Signior Corvino* Mosca mimics Volpone's feeble cry
39 *blind harper* proverbial term for anonymous figure in a crowd
46 *fable* story, report (not 'fiction')

The Dwarf, the Fool, the Eunuch are all his;
He's the true father of his family,
In all, save me: but he has given 'em nothing.

CORVINO
That's well, that's well. Art sure he does not hear us? 50

MOSCA
Sure, sir? Why, look you, credit your own sense.

[*Shouts in* VOLPONE'S *ear*]

The pox approach, and add to your diseases,
If it would send you hence the sooner, sir,
For, your incontinence, it hath deserved it
Throughly and throughly, and the plague to boot. 55
[*To* CORVINO] You may come near, sir.
Would you once close
Those filthy eyes of yours, that flow with slime,
Like two frog-pits; and those same hanging cheeks,
Covered with hide instead of skin—Nay, help, sir—
That look like frozen dish-clouts, set on end. 60

CORVINO
Or, like an old smoked wall, on which the rain
Ran down in streaks.

MOSCA
Excellent, sir, speak out;
You may be louder yet; a culverin
Dischargèd in his ear, would hardly bore it.

CORVINO
His nose is like a common sewer, still running. 65

MOSCA
'Tis good! And what his mouth?

CORVINO
A very draught.

MOSCA
O, stop it up— [*Starts to smother him*]

CORVINO
By no means.

MOSCA
Pray you, let me.
Faith, I could stifle him, rarely, with a pillow,
As well as any woman that should keep him.

48 *family* household
52 *pox* the great pox, syphilis
54 *it . . . it* 'your incontinence hath deserved the pox'
63 *culverin* hand-gun
66 *draught* sink, cesspool
68 *rarely* excellently
69 *keep* keep house for, look after

CORVINO
Do as you will, but I'll be gone.
MOSCA Be so; 70
It is your presence makes him last so long.
CORVINO
I pray you, use no violence.
MOSCA No, sir? why?
Why should you be thus scrupulous, pray you, sir?
CORVINO
Nay, at your discretion.
MOSCA Well, good sir, be gone.
CORVINO
I will not trouble him now, to take my pearl? 75
MOSCA
Puh! nor your diamant. What a needless care
Is this afflicts you! [*Takes the jewels*] Is not all, here, yours?
Am not I here? whom you have made? your creature?
That owe my being to you?
CORVINO Grateful Mosca!
Thou art my friend, my fellow, my companion, 80
My partner, and shalt share in all my fortunes.
MOSCA
Excepting one.
CORVINO What's that?
MOSCA Your gallant wife, sir.
[*Exit* CORVINO]
Now, is he gone; we had no other means
To shoot him hence, but this.
VOLPONE My divine Mosca!
Thou hast today outgone thyself. *Another knocks*
Who's there? 85
I will be troubled with no more. Prepare
Me music, dances, banquets, all delights;
The Turk is not more sensual in his pleasures
Than will Volpone. [*Exit* MOSCA] Let me see, a pearl!
A diamant! plate! chequeens! Good morning's purchase; 90
Why, this is better than rob churches, yet;
Or fat, by eating, once a month, a man. [*Enter* MOSCA]
Who is't?
MOSCA The beauteous Lady Would-be, sir,

75 *pearl* this, with the diamond, is still in Volpone's fist
82 *gallant* fine, beautiful
90 *purchase* haul (thieves' cant)

Wife, to the English knight, Sir Politic Would-be,
(This is the style, sir, is directed me) 95
Hath sent to know, how you have slept tonight,
And if you would be visited.

VOLPONE
Not now.
Some three hours hence—

MOSCA
I told the squire so much.

VOLPONE
When I am high with mirth, and wine: then, then.
'Fore heaven, I wonder at the desperate valour 100
Of the bold English, that they dare let loose
Their wives, to all encounters!

MOSCA
Sir, this knight
Had not his name for nothing, he is politic,
And knows, how e'er his wife affect strange airs,
She hath not yet the face, to be dishonest. 105
But, had she Signior Corvino's wife's face—

VOLPONE
Has she so rare a face?

MOSCA
O, sir, the wonder,
The blazing star of Italy! a wench
O' the first year, a beauty, ripe, as harvest!
Whose skin is whiter than a swan, all over! 110
Than silver, snow, or lillies! a soft lip,
Would tempt you to eternity of kissing!
And flesh that melteth, in the touch, to blood!
Bright as your gold! and lovely as your gold!

VOLPONE
Why had I not known this before?

MOSCA
Alas, sir, 115
Myself, but yesterday, discovered it.

VOLPONE
How might I see her?

MOSCA
O, not possible;
She's kept as warily as is your gold;
Never does come abroad, never takes air

100 *desperate valour* the English were much wondered at in Italy for the freedom they allowed their wives; the Italians were reputed to incarcerate them (see below, pp. 162–3)
105 *dishonest* unchaste
109 *O'the first year* perhaps 'without blemish'; see *Leviticus* IX. iii, XII. vi etc., referring to the sacrificial kid or lamb; but perhaps 'young and tender'
119 *abroad* out of the house

But at a window. All her looks are sweet, 120
As the first grapes, or cherries, and are watched
As near as they are.

VOLPONE I must see her—

MOSCA Sir,
There is a guard, of ten spies thick, upon her;
All his whole household: each of which is set
Upon his fellow, and have all their charge, 125
When he goes out, when he comes in, examined.

VOLPONE
I will go see her, though but at her window.

MOSCA
In some disguise, then.

VOLPONE That is true. I must
Maintain mine own shape, still, the same; we'll think.

[*Exeunt* VOLPONE, MOSCA]

Act II, Scene i

[*The Square, before* CORVINO'S *House*)
[*Enter*] POLITIC WOULD-BE, PEREGRINE

SIR POLITIC
Sir, to a wise man, all the world's his soil.
It is not Italy, nor France, nor Europe,
That must bound me, if my fates call me forth.
Yet, I protest, it is no salt desire
Of seeing countries, shifting a religion, 5
Nor any disaffection to the state
Where I was bred (and unto which I owe
My dearest plots) hath brought me out; much less
That idle, antique, stale, grey-headed project
Of knowing men's minds, and manners, with Ulysses; 10
But a peculiar humour of my wife's,

120 *window* ed. (FQ windore); Jonson's spelling was based on the false derivation 'wind-door'; the s.d. at II. ii, 222 has *windo'* in F, suggesting that the pronunciation was as now
122 *near* closely
125–126 *charge . . . examined* i.e. each is questioned about the servant under his charge
129 *mine own shape* i.e. his own apparent shape
4 *salt* wanton (used of bitches on heat)
8 *plots* projects
10 *knowing . . . Ulysses* alluding to the first lines of the *Odyssey*
11 *humour* whim, obsession

Laid for this height of Venice, to observe,
To quote, to learn the language, and so forth—
I hope you travel, sir, with licence?

PEREGRINE Yes.

SIR POLITIC
I dare the safelier converse—How long, sir, 15
Since you left England?

PEREGRINE Seven weeks.

SIR POLITIC So lately!
You ha' not been with my lord ambassador?

PEREGRINE
Not yet, sir.

SIR POLITIC Pray you, what news, sir, vents our climate?
I heard, last night, a most strange thing reported
By some of my lord's followers, and I long 20
To hear, how 'twill be seconded.

PEREGRINE What was't, sir?

SIR POLITIC
Marry, sir, of a raven, that should build
In a ship royal of the King's.

PEREGRINE [*Aside*]—This fellow
Does he gull me, trow? or is gulled?—Your name, sir?

SIR POLITIC
My name is Politic Would-be.

PEREGRINE [*Aside*]—O, that speaks him— 25
A knight, sir?

SIR POLITIC A poor knight, sir.

PEREGRINE Your lady
Lies here, in Venice, for intelligence
Of tires, and fashions, and behaviour
Among the courtesans? The fine Lady Would-be?

12 *Laid for this height* setting course for this latitude
13 *quote* make notes
14 *licence* warrant from the Lords of Council
17 *my lord ambassador* Sir Henry Wotton was ambassador to Venice from 1604 to 1612; Sir Politic has been thought to caricature him (see Introduction p. xix)
18 *vents* 'comes out of' or 'publishes'; the rhetoric strains either usage
22 *should* 'it is said', from an Old English usage
24 *gull* take in, fool (see Prologue 23n.)
25 *speaks him* expresses what he is
27 *Lies* stays
28 *tires* attires, head-dresses

SIR POLITIC
Yes, sir, the spider, and the bee, oft-times, 30
Suck from one flower.

PEREGRINE Good Sir Politic!
I cry your mercy; I have heard much of you:
'Tis true, sir, of your raven.

SIR POLITIC On your knowledge?

PEREGRINE
Yes, and your lions whelping, in the Tower.

SIR POLITIC
Another whelp!

PEREGRINE Another, sir.

SIR POLITIC Now, heaven! 35
What prodigies be these? The fires at Berwick!
And the new star! These things concurring, strange!
And full of omen! Saw you those meteors?

PEREGRINE
I did, sir.

SIR POLITIC Fearful! Pray you sir, confirm me,
Were there three porcpisces seen, above the bridge, 40
As they give out?

PEREGRINE Six, and a sturgeon, sir.

SIR POLITIC
I am astonished!

PEREGRINE Nay, sir, be not so;
I'll tell you a greater prodigy, than these—

SIR POLITIC
What should these things portend!

32 *I cry your mercy* I beg your pardon

33 *On your knowledge* 'your' may be impersonal, 'This is known to be true?'

35 *Another whelp!* Stow's *Annals* reports the whelping of King James's lions in the Tower on 5 August 1604 and 26 February 1605

36 *fires at Berwick* ghostly battles on Halidon Hill near Berwick caused border alarms in 1604; aurora borealis has been suggested as contributory to this and other marvels of the time

37 *the new star* Kepler discovered a nova in constellation Serpens in 1604; it was brighter than Jupiter and disappeared after two years

38 *meteors* taken as ill omens, because an apparent disturbance of the cosmos

40 *porcpisces* Jonson's spelling is retained with its correct etymology; Stow tells of 'a great Porpus' taken from the Thames, and of 'a very great whale' up river a few days later (*Annals* 19 Jan. 1605/6); for the dating of the play see Introduction p. xxvii

PEREGRINE The very day
(Let me be sure) that I put forth from London, 45
There was a whale discovered, in the river,
As high as Woolwich, that had waited there,
Few know how many months, for the subversion
Of the Stode fleet.

SIR POLITIC Is't possible? Believe it,
'Twas either sent from Spain, or the Archdukes! 50
Spinola's whale, upon my life, my credit!
Will they not leave these projects? Worthy sir,
Some other news.

PEREGRINE Faith, Stone the fool is dead,
And they do lack a tavern fool, extremely.

SIR POLITIC
Is Mas' Stone dead?

PEREGRINE He's dead, sir; why? I hope 55
You thought him not immortal? [*Aside*]—O, this knight,
Were he well known, would be a precious thing
To fit our English stage: he that should write
But such a fellow, should be thought to feign
Extremely, if not maliciously.

SIR POLITIC Stone dead! 60

PEREGRINE
Dead. Lord! how deeply, sir, you apprehend it!
He was no kinsman to you?

SIR POLITIC That I know of.
Well! that same fellow was an unknown fool.

49 *Stode fleet* the English Merchant Adventurers were displaced from Hamburg and settled at Stade (Stode) at the mouth of the Elbe

50 *Archdukes* F (Q Arch-duke); the F reading may be the possessive (Archduke's) or it may be the correct style for Isabella and Albert, joint rulers of the Spanish Netherlands

51 *Spinola* commander of the Spanish army in the Netherlands, often credited by the gullible with monstrous ingenuity; he was said to have hired a whale to drown London 'by snuffing up the Thames and spouting it upon the City'

53 *Stone* in the spring of 1605 'Stone the fool' was whipped in Bridewell for 'a blasphemous speech' in which he called the Lord Admiral a fool

55 *Mas'* master

61 *apprehend* both 'feel' and 'understand'

62 *That I know of* 'not' understood before 'that'

63 *unknown* i.e. not known for what he really was

PEREGRINE
And yet you knew him, it seems?
SIR POLITIC I did so. Sir,
I knew him one of the most dangerous heads 65
Living within the state, and so I held him.
PEREGRINE
Indeed, sir?
SIR POLITIC While he lived, in action.
He has received weekly intelligence,
Upon my knowledge, out of the Low Countries,
For all parts of the world, in cabbages; 70
And those dispensed, again, t'ambassadors,
In oranges, musk-melons, apricots,
Lemons, pome-citrons, and such-like: sometimes
In Colchester oysters, and your Selsey cockles.
PEREGRINE
You make me wonder!
SIR POLITIC Sir, upon my knowledge. 75
Nay, I have observed him, at your public ordinary,
Take his advertisement, from a traveller
(A concealed statesman) in a trencher of meat;
And, instantly, before the meal was done,
Convey an answer in a toothpick.
PEREGRINE Strange! 80
How could this be, sir?
SIR POLITIC Why, the meat was cut
So like his character, and so laid, as he
Must easily read the cipher.
PEREGRINE I have heard,
He could not read, sir.
SIR POLITIC So 'twas given out,
In polity, by those that did employ him: 85

64 *you knew him* F (Q you know him); the Q reading would make Sir Politic's retort portentously pedantic and may therefore be preferred
70 *cabbages* regularly imported from Holland at this time
72 *musk-melons* common melons
73 *pome-citrons* citrons, or limes
74 *Colchester oysters . . . Selsey cockles* both delicacies in court circles
76 *ordinary* tavern offering fixed prices
77 *advertisement* instruction or information
78 *concealed statesman* disguised agent of state
82 *character* cipher, code; cutting food into intricate shapes was fashionable, see *Cymbeline* IV. ii, 49

But he could read, and had your languages,
And to't, as sound a noddle—

PEREGRINE I have heard, sir,
That your baboons were spies; and that they were
A kind of subtle nation, near to China.

SIR POLITIC
Ay, ay, your *Mamuluchi*. Faith, they had 90
Their hand in a French plot, or two; but they
Were so extremely given to women, as
They made discovery of all: yet I
Had my advices here, on Wednesday last,
From one of their own coat, they were returned, 95
Made their relations, as the fashion is,
And now stand fair, for fresh employment.

PEREGRINE [*Aside*]—'Heart!
This Sir Pol will be ignorant of nothing—
It seems, sir, you know all?

SIR POLITIC Not all, sir. But,
I have some general notions; I do love 100
To note, and to observe: though I live out,
Free from the active torrent, yet I'd mark
The currents, and the passages of things,
For mine own private use; and know the ebbs,
And flows of state.

PEREGRINE Believe it, sir, I hold 105
Myself, in no small tie, unto my fortunes
For casting me thus luckily, upon you;
Whose knowledge, if your bounty equal it,
May do me great assistance, in instruction
For my behaviour, and my bearing, which 110
Is yet so rude, and raw.

SIR POLITIC Why? came you forth
Empty of rules for travel?

87 *noddle* the back of the head and seat of the mind; perhaps less playful here than in its common use
90 *Mamuluchi* a macaronic version of *mamalik*, Circassian slaves who came to rule Egypt in the thirteenth century; nothing to do with baboons or China
93 *discovery* disclosure
94 *advices* news, dispatches
95 *coat* side
96 *relations* reports
97 *stand fair* are well set
97 *'Heart* i.e. God's Heart!
106 *tie* obligation

PEREGRINE Faith, I had
Some common ones, from out that vulgar grammar,
Which he that cried Italian to me, taught me.

SIR POLITIC
Why, this it is, that spoils all our brave bloods; 115
Trusting our hopeful gentry unto pedants:
Fellows of outside, and mere bark. You seem
To be a gentleman, of ingenuous race—
I not profess it, but my fate hath been
To be, where I have been consulted with, 120
In this high kind, touching some great men's sons,
Persons of blood, and honour—

PEREGRINE [*Seeing people approach*] Who be these, sir?

Act II, Scene ii

[*Enter* MOSCA *and* NANO, *disguised, with materials for a scaffold stage. A crowd follows.*]

MOSCA
Under that window, there't must be. The same.

SIR POLITIC
Fellows, to mount a bank! Did your instructor
In the dear tongues, never discourse to you
Of the Italian mountebanks?

PEREGRINE Yes, sir.

SIR POLITIC Why,
Here shall you see one.

PEREGRINE They are quacksalvers, 5
Fellows, that live by venting oils and drugs?

SIR POLITIC
Was that the character he gave you of them?

113 *vulgar grammar* ordinary grammar book, apt to contain phrases and precepts; Florio's grammar may be intended
114 *cried* called out, intoned
117 *bark* shell, outward appearance; may include pun suggested by 'cried'
118 *ingenuous* noble; Sir Politic pauses to weigh Peregrine's potential
121 *high kind* important capacity
s.d. *scaffold stage* see Introduction pp. xxviii–xxix
2 *mount a bank* from Italian *monta in banco*; *bank* bench; see p. 164
3 *dear* esteemed
5 *quacksalvers* a Dutch word for quackers about ointment; hence modern 'quack'
6 *venting* vending

PEREGRINE
As I remember.

SIR POLITIC Pity his ignorance.
They are the only knowing men of Europe!
Great general scholars, excellent physicians, 10
Most admired statesmen, professed favourites,
And cabinet counsellors, to the greatest princes!
The only languaged men, of all the world!

PEREGRINE
And, I have heard, they are most lewd impostors;
Made all of terms, and shreds; no less beliers 15
Of great men's favours, than their own vile medicines;
Which they will utter, upon monstrous oaths:
Selling that drug, for twopence, ere they part,
Which they have valued at twelve crowns, before.

SIR POLITIC
Sir, calumnies are answered best with silence: 20
Yourself shall judge. Who is it mounts, my friends?

MOSCA
Scoto of Mantua, sir.

SIR POLITIC Is't he? Nay, then
I'll proudly promise, sir, you shall behold
Another man, than has been phant'sied to you.
I wonder, yet, that he should mount his bank 25
Here, in this nook, that has been wont t'appear
In face of the Piazza! Here, he comes.

[*Enter* VOLPONE, *as a mountebank; with a crowd*]

LX 12

14 *lewd* ignorant 15 *terms, and shreds* jargon, snatches and tags
15 *beliers* misreporters 17 *utter* sell (compare Epistle, 69 and note)
22 *Scoto of Mantua* renowned Italian juggler who visited Elizabeth's court in 1576
27 *In face of* facing on to

---

27 *Enter* VOLPONE. A. B. Kernan finds a number of parallels between Volpone's Scoto and Jonson's professional situation. Both are playing before a popular audience after being used to a fashionable one (for all Jonson's plays were at Blackfriars before *Sejanus* and *Volpone* appeared at the Globe); Jonson was imprisoned because *Eastward Ho* offended King James, while Scoto is rumoured to have suffered the galleys for offending Cardinal Bembo; both aspire to learning and share a contempt for public taste; and it may be that the sixpence charged for the elixir was the cost of the more expensive seats at the first performance of *Volpone*. It is quite probable that Jonson glances archly and sardonically at his own art as public entertainer, but this is not (of course) the main effect of the scene.

VOLPONE [*to* NANO]
Mount, zany.

CROWD Follow, follow, follow, follow, follow.

SIR POLITIC
See how the people follow him! He's a man
May write ten thousand crowns, in bank, here. Note, 30
Mark but his gesture: I do use to observe
The state he keeps, in getting up! [VOLPONE *mounts stage*]

PEREGRINE 'Tis worth it, sir.

VOLPONE
Most noble gentlemen, and my worthy patrons, it may seem strange, that I, your Scoto Mantuano, who was ever wont to fix my bank in face of the public Piazza, near the 35 shelter of the Portico to the Procuratia, should, now, after eight months' absence, from this illustrious city of Venice humbly retire myself, into an obscure nook of the Piazza.

SIR POLITIC
Did not I, now, object the same?

PEREGRINE Peace, sir.

VOLPONE
Let me tell you: I am not, as your Lombard proverb saith, 40 cold on my feet, or content to part with my commodities at a cheaper rate, than I accustomed: look not for it. Nor, that the calumnious reports of that impudent detractor, and shame to our profession—Alessandro Buttone, I mean—who gave out, in public, I was condemned *a sforzato* to the 45 galleys, for poisoning the Cardinal Bembo's—cook, hath at all attached, much less dejected me. No, no, worthy gentlemen, to tell you true, I cannot endure, to see the rabble of these ground *ciarlitani*, that spread their cloaks on the pavement, as if they meant to do feats of activity, and 50

28 *zany* clown and servant, comic assistant
36 *Portico to the Procuratia* the arcaded residence of the Procurators on the north side of St. Mark's
39 *object* possibly in archaic sense 'put before the mind'
41 *cold on my feet* Italian, *aver freddo a 'piedi*, i.e. to be forced by poverty to sell cheaply
44 *Buttone* the name of this rival owes nothing to fact
45 *sforzato* '*Sfortzati*, gallie-slaves, prisoners perforce' (Florio 1598)
46 *Bembo's—cook* the pause insinuates 'mistress'; Pietro Bembo (1470–1547), the great humanist, was born in Venice
47 *attached* arrested, constrained
49 *ground ciarlitani* charlatans working on the ground, without a bank

then come in, lamely, with their mouldy tales out of Boccaccio, like stale Tabarine, the fabulist: some of them discoursing their travels, and of their tedious captivity in the Turk's galleys, when indeed, were the truth known, they were the Christian's galleys, where very temperately, they ate bread, and drunk water, as a wholesome penance, enjoined them by their confessors, for base pilferies. 55

SIR POLITIC

Note but his bearing, and contempt of these.

VOLPONE

These turdy-facy-nasty-paty-lousy-fartical rogues, with one poor groat's-worth of unprepared antimony, finely wrapped up in several *scartoccios*, are able, very well, to kill their twenty a week, and play; yet, these meagre starved spirits, who have half stopped the organs of their minds with earthy oppilations, want not their favourers among your shrivelled, salad-eating artisans: who are overjoyed, that they may have their half-pe'rth of physic, though it purge 'em into another world, 't makes no matter. 60 65

SIR POLITIC

Excellent! Ha' you heard better language, sir?

VOLPONE

Well, let 'em go. And gentlemen, honourable gentlemen, know, that for this time, our bank, being thus removed from the clamours of the *canaglia*, shall be the scene of pleasure, and delight; for, I have nothing to sell, little, or nothing to sell. 70

SIR POLITIC

I told you, sir, his end.

PEREGRINE You did so, sir.

VOLPONE

I protest, I, and my six servants, are not able to make of this 75

52 *Tarbarine* a famous zany in a touring Italian troop of the 1570s
56 *ate* (FQ eate)
59 *turdy . . . fartical* an Aristophanic phrase, compounded of abusive improvisations
61 *several* separate
61 *scartoccios* 'a coffin of paper for spice' (Florio 1598)
64 *earthly oppilations* gross obstructions, i.e. mundane concerns
65 *salad* probably meaning 'raw vegetables'
66 *half-pe'rth* ha'p'orth
71 *canaglia* 'raskallie people onelie fit for dogs companie' (Florio 1598)

precious liquor, so fast, as it is fetched away from my lodgings by gentlemen of your city; strangers of the Terra Firma; worshipful merchants; ay, and senators too: who, ever since my arrival, have detained me to their uses, by their splendidous liberalities. And worthily. For, what avails your rich man to have his magazines stuffed with *moscadelli*, or of the purest grape, when his physicians prescribe him, on pain of death, to drink nothing but water, cocted with aniseeds? O, health! health! the blessing of the rich! the riches of the poor! who can buy thee at too dear a rate, since there is no enjoying this world without thee? Be not then so sparing of your purses, honourable gentlemen, as to abridge the natural course of life— 80 85

PEREGRINE
You see his end?

SIR POLITIC
Ay, is't not good?

VOLPONE
For, when a humid flux, or catarrh, by the mutability of air, falls from your head, into an arm, or shoulder, or any other part; take you a ducat, or your chequeen of gold, and apply to the place affected: see, what good effect it can work. No, no, 'tis this blessed *unguento*, this rare extraction, that hath only power to disperse all malignant humours, that proceed, either of hot, cold, moist, or windy causes— 90 95

PEREGRINE
I would he had put in dry too.

SIR POLITIC
Pray you, observe.

77–78 *Terra Firma* name for the mainland part of Venice
80 *splendidous* common variant of 'splendid'
81 *magazines* storehouses
81 *moscadelli* 'the wine Muscadine' (Florio 1598), muscatel
83 *cocted* boiled 94 *unguento* ointment

95 *malignant humours*. According to classical and medieval medical theory the four cardinal humours of the body were blood, phlegm, choler and melancholy, and they corresponded with the four elements—air (hot and moist), water (cold and moist), fire (hot and dry) and earth (cold and dry). Both pathological and temperamental traits were attributed to the dominance of one humour over the others, or to 'fluxes'—flowings of humours from one part of the body to another. In his early 'Humour' plays Jonson made some use of the psychological or character-forming aspect of the theory, but in *Volpone* it is confined to pathology; the notion that a man can fall under the dominion of a single passion or obsession, however, remains crucial, for upon it depends one's sense of the reality of Jonson's figures.

VOLPONE

To fortify the most indigest, and crude stomach, ay, were it of one that, through extreme weakness, vomited blood, applying only a warm napkin to the place, after the unction, 100 and fricace; for the *vertigine*, in the head, putting but a drop into your nostrils, likewise, behind the ears; a most sovereign, and approved remedy: the *mal caduco*, cramps, convulsions, paralyses, epilepsies, *tremor-cordia*, retired nerves, ill vapours of the spleen, stoppings of the liver, the stone, the 105 strangury, *hernia ventosa*, *iliaca passio*; stops a *disenteria* immediately; easeth the tortion of the small guts; and cures *melancholia hypocondriaca*, being taken and applied, according to my printed receipt. (*Pointing to his bill and his glass*) For, this is the physician, this the medicine; this 110 counsels, this cures; this gives the direction, this works the effect: and, in sum, both together may be termed an abstract of the theoric, and practic in the Aesculapian art. 'Twill cost you eight crowns. And, Zan Fritada, pray thee sing a verse, extempore, in honour of it. 115

SIR POLITIC

How do you like him, sir?

PEREGRINE

Most strangely, I!

SIR POLITIC

Is not his language rare?

PEREGRINE

But alchemy,
I never heard the like: or Broughton's books.

98 *crude* sour 101 *fricace* massage
101 *vertigine* dizziness
103 *mal caduco* falling sickness (epilepsy)
104 *tremor-cordia* heart palpitations
104 *retired nerves* shrunken sinews
106 *strangury* painful urination
106 *hernia ventosa* gaseous protrusion (possibly strangulated hernia)
106 *iliaca passio* 'pain and wringing of the small guts (Holland's *Pliny* II. 39)
108 *melancholia hypocondriaca* melancholy was supposed to be seated in the hypochondria—the soft parts of the body below the rib cartilages 109 *receipt* recipe
113 *Aesculapian* after Aesculapius, Greek and Roman god of medicine
114 *Zan Fritada* Volpone calls Nano by the name of a celebrated zany (*fritata* = pancake) 117 *But* 'except for' or 'pure'
118 *Broughton* Hugh Broughton (1549–1612), rabbinical scholar and Puritan; compare *The Alchemist* II. iii, 237 where Doll's madness (IV. v, 1–32) is blamed on Broughton

[NANO *sings*]

Song

Had old Hippocrates, or Galen, 120
That to their books put medicines all in,
But known this secret, they had never
(Of which they will be guilty ever)
Been murderers of so much paper,
Or wasted many a hurtless taper: 125
No Indian drug had ere been famèd,
Tobacco, sassafras not namèd,
Ne yet of guacum one small stick, sir,
Nor Raymond Lully's great elixir.
Ne had been known the Danish Gonswart, 130
Or Paracelsus, with his long sword.

PEREGRINE
All this, yet, will not do; eight crowns is high.

VOLPONE
No more; gentlemen, if I had but time to discourse to you the miraculous effects of this my oil, surnamed *oglio del Scoto*; with the countless catalogue of those I have cured of 135 th'aforsaid, and many more diseases; the patents and privileges of all the princes and commonwealths of Christendom; or but the depositions of those that appeared on my part, before the signiory of the *Sanita*, and most learned college of physicians; where I was authorized, upon 140 notice taken of the admirable virtues of my medicaments,

120 *Hippocrates, or Galen* Hippocrates (born *c.* 460 BC) invented the theory of humours and Galen (born *c.* AD 130) expounded it; their authority in all medical matters was still recognised in Jonson's time

125 *hurtless* harmless

127 *Tobacco, sassafras* both used medicinally and newly introduced from America

128 *guacum* drug extracted from resin of guaiacum tree

129 *Raymond Lully* (1235–1315) sage, evangelist, and astrologer from Majorca; apocryphal alchemical works were ascribed to him posthumously, hence the tradition that he discovered the elixir of life; see *The Alchemist* II. v, 8

130 *Danish Gonswart* unidentified; suggestions include a Dutch theologian (Wessel Gansfort) and a Danish Chemist (Berthold Schwarz)

131 *Paracelsus . . . sword* Paracelsus was supposed to have kept his quintessences in the pommel of his sword

139 *signiory of the Sanita* the 'health masters' of Venice who licensed physicians, drug-vendors and mountebanks

and mine own excellency, in matter of rare, and unknown
secrets, not only to dispense them publicly in this famous
city, but in all the territories, that happily joy under the
government of the most pious and magnificent states of 145
Italy. But may some other gallant fellow say, 'O, there be
divers that make profession to have as good, and as
experimented receipts as yours.' Indeed, very many have
assayed, like apes in imitation of that, which is really and
essentially in me, to make of this oil; bestowed great cost 150
in furnaces, stills, alembics, continual fires and preparation
of the ingredients (as indeed there goes to it six hundred
several simples, besides some quantity of human fat, for the
conglutination, which we buy of the anatomists) but, when
these practitioners come to the last decoction, blow, blow, 155
puff, puff, and all flies *in fumo*: ha, ha, ha! Poor wretches! I
rather pity their folly, and indiscretion, than their loss of
time, and money; for those may be recovered by industry:
but to be a fool born, is a disease incurable. For my self, I
always from my youth have endeavoured to get the rarest 160
secrets, and book them; either in exchange, or for money: I
spared not cost, nor labour, where anything was worthy to
be learned. And gentlemen, honourable gentlemen, I will
undertake, by virtue of chemical art, out of the honourable
hat, that covers your head, to extract the four elements; 165
that is to say, the fire, air, water, and earth, and return you
your felt without burn, or stain. For, whilst others have
been at the balloo, I have been at my book; and am now
past the craggy paths of study, and come to the flowery
plains of honour, and reputation. 170

SIR POLITIC

I do assure you, sir, that is his aim.

VOLPONE

But, to our price—

PEREGRINE And that withall, Sir Pol.

VOLPONE

You all know, honourable gentlemen, I never valued this
ampulla, or vial, at less than eight crowns, but for this time,

151 *alembics* alchemical stills
153 *several* separate
153 *simples* remedies made from one herb only
155 *decoction* boiling down to extract essences
155 *blow, blow* imitates the alchemist at his furnace
168 *balloo* (balloon) Venetian game; see p. 163
174 *ampulla* 'a thin viole-glasse' (Florio 1598)

I am content to be deprived of it for six; six crowns is the price; and less in courtesy, I know you cannot offer me: take it, or leave it, howsoever, both it, and I, am at your service. I ask you not, as the value of the thing, for then I should demand of you a thousand crowns, so the Cardinals Montalto, Fernese, the great Duke of Tuscany, my gossip, with divers other princes have given me; but I despise money: only to show my affection to you, honourable gentlemen, and your illustrious state here, I have neglected the messages of these princes, mine own offices, framed my journey hither, only to present you with the fruits of my travels. [*To* NANO *and* MOSCA] Tune your voices once more to the touch of your instruments, and give the honourable assembly some delightful recreation. 175 180 185

PEREGRINE

What monstrous, and most painful circumstance
Is here, to get some three or four *gazets*! 190
Some threepence, i' th' whole, for that 'twill come to.

Song

You that would last long, list to my song,
Make no more coil, but buy of this oil.
Would you be ever fair? and young? 195
Stout of teeth? and strong of tongue?
Tart of palate? quick of ear?
Sharp of sight? of nostril clear?
Moist of hand? and light of foot?
Or, I will come nearer to it, 200
Would you live free from all diseases?
Do the act, your mistress pleases;

179–180 *Cardinals Montalto, Fernese* Montalto became Pope Sixtus V in 1585; *Fernese* probably an allusion to the notorious Alessandro Farnese who became Pope Paul III in 1534 but there was also a later Cardinal Alessandro Farnese (1520–1589)
180 *Duke of Tuscany* office held by Cosimo de' Medici after 1569
180 *gossip* godsib, godfather; also 'familiar acquaintance'
184 *offices* duties
189 *What monstrous . . .* Peregrine's speech is probably aside to the audience
190 *gazets* Venetian pennies, as Peregrine's explanation indicates
194 *coil* pother, fuss
197 *Tart* sharp, keen
199 *Moist of hand* the sign of 'pith and livelihood' in *Venus & Adonis* 25–26

Yet fright all aches from your bones?
Here's a medicine, for the nones.

VOLPONE

Well, I am in a humour, at this time, to make a present of the small quantity my coffer contains: to the rich, in courtesy, and to the poor, for God's sake. Wherefore, now mark; I asked you six crowns; and six crowns, at other times, you have paid me; you shall not give me six crowns, nor five, nor four, nor three, nor two, nor one; nor half a ducat; no, nor a *moccenigo*: six—pence it will cost you, or six hundred pound—expect no lower price, for by the banner of my front, I will not bate a *bagatine*, that I will have, only, a pledge of your loves, to carry something from amongst you, to show, I am not contemned by you. Therefore, now, toss your handkerchiefs, cheerfully, cheerfully; and be advertised, that the first heroic spirit, that deigns to grace me, with a handkerchief, I will give it a little remembrance of something, beside, shall please it better, than if I had presented it with a double pistolet. 205 210 215 220

PEREGRINE

Will you be that heroic spark, Sir Pol?
O, see! the window has prevented you.

CELIA *at the window throws down her handkerchief*

VOLPONE

Lady, I kiss your bounty: and for this timely grace, you have done your poor Scoto of Mantua, I will return you,

203 *aches . . . bones* probably alluding to venereal disease, the 'incurable bone-ache' of *Troilus & Cressida* V. i, 21; 'aches' pronounced as disyllable
204 *nones* nonce, occasion
211 *moccenigo* 'a kind of coine in Venice' (Florio 1598) perhaps worth nine *gazets*
212–213 *banner of my front* displayed upon the scaffold, listing maladies and cures
213 *bate* abate
213 *bagatine* 'a little coine in Italie' (Florio 1598) about a third of a farthing
216 *handkerchiefs* i.e. with the money knotted into a corner; the usual practice
218 *give it* i.e. the heroic spirit
220 *pistolet* Spanish gold coin, then worth about eighteen shillings
221 *spark* gallant, brave fellow
222 s.d. *Celia at the window* presumably on the tarras or in the window-stage; the text does not say when she first appears

over and above my oil, a secret of that high, and inestimable 225
nature, shall make you for ever enamoured on that minute,
wherein your eye first descended on so mean, yet not
altogether to be despised, an object. Here is a poulder,
concealed in this paper, of which, if I should speak to the
worth, nine thousand volumes were but as one page, that 230
page as a line, that line as a word: so short is this pilgrimage
of man (which some call life) to the expressing of it. Would
I reflect on the price? Why, the whole world were but as an
empire, that empire as a province, that province as a bank,
that bank as a private purse, to the purchase of it. I will, 235
only, tell you; it is the poulder that made Venus a goddess,
given her by Apollo, that kept her perpetually young, cleared
her wrinkles, firmed her gums, filled her skin, coloured her
hair; from her, derived to Helen, and at the sack of Troy,
unfortunately, lost: till now, in this our age, it was as happily 240
recovered, by a studious antiquary, out of some ruins of Asia,
who sent a moiety of it, to the court of France (but much
sophisticated), wherewith the ladies there, now, colour their
hair. The rest, at this present, remains with me; extracted to
a quintessence: so that, wherever it but touches, in youth it 245
perpetually preserves, in age restores the complexion; seats
your teeth, did they dance like virginal jacks, firm as a
wall; makes them white, as ivory, that were black, as —

Act II, Scene iii

13

[*Enter* CORVINO]

CORVINO

Spite o' the devil, and my shame! come down here;
Come down! No house but mine to make your *scene*?

He beats away the mountebank, &c.

228 *poulder* powder; Jonson preferred this spelling (Latin *pulvis*)
242 *moiety* a half, or a part
243 *sophisticated* adulterated
247 *virginal jacks* strictly the pieces of wood bearing the quills of the virginals, but sometimes erroneously used for keys (the image derives from Rabelais)
1 *Spite o'* F (Q Bloud of); the first part of the line is probably to Celia, and the rest to Volpone; the F reading makes the wife the devil's agent
2 *scene* critical theory prescribed for a 'scene' a public place overlooked by private houses, and window scenes were common in the *commedia dell'arte*

Signior Flaminio, will you down, sir? down!
What, is my wife your Franciscina, sir?
No windows on the whole Piazza, here, 5
To make your properties, but mine? but mine?
Heart! ere tomorrow, I shall be new christened,
And called the *Pantalone di Besogniosi*,
About the town. [*Exit*]

PEREGRINE What should this mean, Sir Pol?

SIR POLITIC
Some trick of state, believe it. I will home. 10

PEREGRINE
It may be some design, on you.

SIR POLITIC I know not.
I'll stand upon my guard.

PEREGRINE It is your best, sir.

SIR POLITIC
This three weeks, all my advices, all my letters,
They have been intercepted.

PEREGRINE Indeed, sir?
Best have a care.

SIR POLITIC Nay, so I will.

PEREGRINE This knight, 15
I may not lose him, for my mirth, till night.

Act II, Scene iv

[VOLPONE'S *house*]

[*Enter*] VOLPONE, MOSCA

VOLPONE
O, I am wounded,

MOSCA Where, sir?

VOLPONE Not without;
Those blows were nothing: I could bear them ever.
But angry Cupid, bolting from her eyes,
Hath shot himself into me, like a flame;

3 *Flaminio* Flaminio Scala, leading figure in the *commedia*, associated with Venice
4 *Franciscina* stock character of maid in the *commedia*
8 *Pantalone di Besogniosi* stock Venetian character in the *commedia*; a lean old man in loose slippers, black cap and gown, and red dress; his name derives him from a line of paupers, and it was often his role to be cuckolded
3 *bolting* darting arrows (bolts)

Where, now, he flings about his burning heat, 5
As in a furnace, an ambitious fire
Whose vent is stopped. The fight is all within me.
I cannot live, except thou help me, Mosca;
My liver melts, and I, without the hope
Of some soft air, from her refreshing breath, 10
Am but a heap of cinders.

MOSCA 'Las, good sir!
Would you had never seen her.

VOLPONE Nay, would thou
Hadst never told me of her.

MOSCA Sir, 'tis true;
I do confess, I was unfortunate,
And you unhappy: but I am bound in conscience, 15
No less than duty, to effect my best
To your release of torment, and I will, sir.

VOLPONE
Dear Mosca, shall I hope?

MOSCA Sir, more than dear,
I will not bid you to despair of ought,
Within a human compass.

VOLPONE O, there spoke 20
My better Angel. Mosca, take my keys,
Gold, plate and jewels, all's at thy devotion;
Employ them, how thou wilt; nay, coin me, too:
So thou, in this, but crown my longings.—Mosca?

MOSCA
Use but your patience.

VOLPONE So I have.

MOSCA I doubt not 25
To bring success to your desires.

VOLPONE Nay, then,
I not repent me of my late disguise.

MOSCA
If you can horn him, sir, you need not.

VOLPONE True:
Besides, I never meant him for my heir.

6 *ambitious fire* rising, swelling flames, recoiling to find other outlets
9 *liver* believed the seat of intense passions
22 *devotion* disposal, with pun on religious sense
23 *coin me* render me into coin
24 *crown* perfect, with pun on coin
24 *—Mosca?* expressing impatience at Mosca's thoughtful silence
28 *horn him* cuckold him

Is not the colour o' my beard, and eyebrows, 30
To make me known?

MOSCA No jot.

VOLPONE I did it well.

MOSCA
So well, would I could follow you in mine,
With half the happiness; and, yet, I would
Escape your *epilogue.*

VOLPONE But, were they gulled
With a belief, that I was Scoto?

MOSCA Sir, 35
Scoto himself could hardly have distinguished!
I have not time to flatter you, now, we'll part:
And, as I prosper, so applaud my art. [*Exeunt*]

Lx 14
Set 3

Act II, Scene v

[CORVINO's *house*]

[*Enter*] CORVINO, CELIA

CORVINO
Death of mine honour, with the city's fool?
A juggling, tooth-drawing, prating mountebank?
And at a public window? where, whilst he,
With his strained action, and his dole of faces,
To his drug lectures draws your itching ears, 5
A crew of old, unmarried, noted lechers
Stood leering up, like satyrs: and you smile
Most graciously! and fan your favours forth,
To give your hot spectators satisfaction!
What, was your mountebank their call? their whistle? 10
Or were you enamoured on his copper rings?
His saffron jewel, with the toad-stone in't?

30 *colour* i.e. the fox's colour, red
32 *mine* i.e. 'my art' (of disguise and mimicry)
33 *happiness* felicitous aptitude
34 *your epilogue* i.e. the beating, but may hint at the end of Mosca's plot
2 *tooth-drawing* the responsibility of mountebanks and barbers
4 *strained action* extravagant gesture
4 *dole of faces* mean repertory of expressions
10 *call . . . whistle* alluding to the enticement of game-fowl
12 *toad-stone* believed to lie between the toad's eyes and to have magical and restorative properties (see *As You Like It* II. i, 12–14)

Or his embroidered suit, with the cope-stitch,
Made of a hearse-cloth? or his old tilt-feather?
Or his starched beard? Well! you shall have him, yes. 15
He shall come home, and minister unto you
The fricace, for the mother. Or, let me see,
I think, you'd rather mount? Would you not mount?
Why, if you'll mount, you may; yes truly, you may:
And so, you may be seen, down to th' foot. 20
Get you a cittern, Lady Vanity,
And be a dealer, with the virtuous man;
Make one: I'll but protest myself a cuckold,
And save your dowry. I am a Dutchman, I!
For, if you thought me an Italian, 25
You would be damned, ere you did this, you whore:
Thou'dst tremble, to imagine, that the murder
Of father, mother, brother, all thy race,
Should follow, as the subject of my justice.

CELIA
Good sir, have patience!

CORVINO What couldst thou propose 30
Less to thyself, than, in this heat of wrath,
And stung with my dishonour, I should strike

[*Takes his sword*]

This steel into thee, with as many stabs,
As thou wert gazed upon with goatish eyes?

13 *cope-stitch* used to decorate a cope border
14 *hearse-cloth* coffin drapery, here either cheap or stolen
14 *tilt-feather* plume worn in tilting helmet; here perhaps found with the hearse-cloth
15 *starched beard* gummed and waxed beards were high fashion
17 *fricace, for the mother* massage for hysteria, believed to be seated in the womb; Corvino puns on suggestions of seduction and birth
18 *mount* i.e. the mountebank's platform, or the mountebank himself; another indecent pun affecting the meaning of 'down to the foot'
21 *cittern* kind of zither or guitar, often carried by a mountebank's wench
21 *Lady Vanity* a character in some morality plays, including that acted in *Sir Thomas More* IV. i
22 *be a dealer* do a deal, trade with (hinting at prostitution)
22 *virtuous man* with sneering pun on 'virtuoso'
23 *Make one* make a deal; mate 23 *protest* declare
24 *save your dowry* an adulteress was deprived of all her inheritance
24 *Dutchman* believed to be long-suffering and phlegmatic

CELIA
Alas sir, be appeased! I could not think 35
My being at the window should more, now,
Move your impatience, than at other times.

CORVINO
No? not to seek, and entertain a parley,
With a known knave? before a multitude?
You were an actor, with your handkerchief! 40
Which he, most sweetly, kissed in the receipt,
And might, no doubt, return it, with a letter,
And point the place, where you might meet: your sister's,
Your mother's, or your aunt's might serve the turn.

CELIA
Why, dear sir, when do I make these excuses? 45
Or ever stir, abroad, but to the church?
And that, so seldom—

CORVINO Well, it shall be less;
And thy restraint, before, was liberty
To what I now decree: and therefore, mark me.
First, I will have this bawdy light dammed up; 50
And, till't be done, some two, or three yards off,
I'll chalk a line; o'er which, if thou but chance
To set thy desp'rate foot; more hell, more horror,
More wild, remorseless rage shall seize on thee,
Than on a conjurer that had heedless left 55
His circle's safety, ere his devil was laid.
Then, here's a lock, which I will hang upon thee;
And, now I think on't, I will keep thee backwards;
Thy lodging shall be backwards; thy walks backwards;
Thy prospect—all be backwards; and no pleasure 60
That thou shalt know, but backwards. Nay, since you force
My honest nature, know it is your own
Being too open, makes me use you thus.
Since you will not contain your subtle nostrils
In a sweet room, but they must snuff the air 65
Of rank, and sweaty passengers—*Knock within*
One knocks.

38 *parley* conversation
50 *light* window
56 *circle* the magician was supposed safe in his circle until the devil was 'laid' to hell
57 *lock* chastity belt
58 *backwards* i.e. at the back of the house
64 *subtle* insidiously acute
66 *passengers* passers-by

Away, and be not seen, pain of thy life;
Not look toward the window: if thou dost—
Nay, stay, hear this; let me not prosper, whore,
But I will make thee an anatomy, 70
Dissect thee mine own self, and read a lecture
Upon thee, to the city, and in public.
Away! [*Exit* CELIA] Who's there? [*Enter* SERVANT]

SERVANT 'Tis Signior Mosca, sir.

Act II, Scene vi

CORVINO
Let him come in, his master's dead. There's yet
Some good, to help the bad. [*Enter* MOSCA] My Mosca, welcome!
I guess your news.

MOSCA I fear you cannot, sir.

CORVINO
Is't not his death?

MOSCA Rather the contrary.

CORVINO
Not his recovery?

MOSCA Yes, sir.

CORVINO I am cursed, 5
I am bewitched, my crosses meet to vex me.
How? how? how? how?

MOSCA Why, sir, with Scoto's oil!
Corbaccio, and Voltore brought of it,
Whilst I was busy in an inner room—

CORVINO
Death! that damned mountebank! But for the law, 10
Now I could kill the rascal: 't cannot be,
His oil should have that virtue. Ha' not I
Known him a common rogue, come fiddling in
To th' *ostería*, with a tumbling whore,
And when he has done all his forced tricks, been glad 15
Of a poor spoonful of dead wine, with flies in 't?

67 *pain* on pain
68 *Not look* do not look
70 *anatomy* body for anatomical demonstration; also moral analysis
6 *crosses* afflictions; with a touch of ironic blasphemy
14 *osteria* inn
14 *tumbling whore* disreputable acrobat (with indecent pun)

It cannot be. All his ingredients
Are a sheep's gall, a roasted bitch's marrow,
Some few sod earwigs, pounded caterpillars,
A little capon's grease, and fasting spittle: 20
I know 'em, to a dram.

MOSCA I know not, sir,
But some on't, there, they poured into his ears,
Some in his nostrils, and recovered him;
Applying but the fricace.

CORVINO Pox o' that fricace.

MOSCA
And since, to seem the more officious, 25
And flattering of his health, there, they have had,
At extreme fees, the college of physicians
Consulting on him, how they might restore him;
Where one would have a cataplasm of spices,
Another, a flayed ape clapped to his breast, 30
A third would ha' it a dog, a fourth an oil
With wild cats' skins: at last, they all resolved
That, to preserve him, was no other means,
But some young woman must be straight sought out,
Lusty, and full of juice, to sleep by him; 35
And, to this service, most unhappily
And most unwillingly, am I now employed,
Which, here, I thought to pre-acquaint you with,
For your advice, since it concerns you most,
Because, I would not do that thing might cross 40
Your ends, on whom I have my whole dependence, sir:
Yet, if I do it not, they may delate
My slackness to my patron, work me out
Of his opinion; and there, all your hopes,
Ventures, or whatsoever, are all frustrate. 45
I do but tell you, sir. Besides, they are all
Now striving, who shall first present him. Therefore—

19 *sod* boiled
20 *fasting spittle* here the saliva of the starving Scoto
25 *officious* dutiful, zealous
27 *extreme fees* the greatest cost
29 *cataplasm* poultice
34 *some young woman* compare the story of David and Abishag (I *Kings* 1)
40–41 *cross Your ends* obstruct your aims 42 *delate* report
47 *present him* i.e. with the young woman
47 *Therefore*— the dash expresses an emphatic pause

I could entreat you, briefly, conclude somewhat:
Prevent 'em if you can.

CORVINO Death to my hopes!
This is my villainous fortune! Best to hire 50
Some common courtesan?

MOSCA Ay, I thought on that, sir.
But they are all so subtle, full of art,
And age again doting, and flexible,
So as—I cannot tell—we may perchance
Light on a quean, may cheat us all.

CORVINO 'Tis true. 55

MOSCA
No, no: it must be one, that has no tricks, sir,
Some simple thing, a creature, made unto it;
Some wench you may command. Ha' you no kinswoman?
God's so—Think, think, think, think, think, think, think, sir.
One o' the doctors offered, there, his daughter. 60

CORVINO
How?

MOSCA Yes, Signior Lupo, the physician.

CORVINO
His daughter!

MOSCA And a virgin, sir. Why, alas
He knows the state of 's body, what it is;
That nought can warm his blood, sir, but a fever;
Nor any incantation raise his spirit; 65
A long forgetfulness hath seized that part.
Besides, sir, who shall know it? some one, or two—

CORVINO
I pray thee give me leave. [*Walks aside*] If any man
But I had had this luck—The thing, in't self,
I know, is nothing—Wherefore should not I 70
As well command my blood, and my affections,
As this dull doctor? In the point of honour,
The cases are all one, of wife, and daughter.

48 *briefly, conclude somewhat* quickly decide something
49 *Prevent 'em* beat 'em to it
53 *again* on the other hand
55 *quean* strumpet
57 *made unto it* made for the part; or possibly 'made to do it' by command
59 *God's so* God's soul; also corruption of *cazzo*, Italian for male organ
61 *Signior Lupo* Mr Wolf; Mosca's invention parodies Jonson's own

MOSCA
[*Aside*] I hear him coming.
CORVINO She shall do't: 'tis done.
'Slight, if this doctor, who is not engaged, 75
Unless 't be for his counsel, which is nothing,
Offer his daughter, what should I, that am
So deeply in? I will prevent him: wretch!
Covetous wretch! Mosca, I have determined.
MOSCA
How, sir?
CORVINO We'll make all sure. The party, you wot of, 80
Shall be mine own wife, Mosca.
MOSCA Sir, the thing,
But that I would not seem to counsel you,
I should have motioned to you, at the first:
And, make your count, you have cut all their throats.
Why! 'tis directly taking a possession! 85
And, in this next fit, we may let him go.
'Tis but to pull the pillow, from his head,
And he is throttled: 't had been done before,
But for your scrupulous doubts.
CORVINO Ay, a plague on't,
My conscience fools my wit. Well, I'll be brief, 90
And so be thou, lest they should be before us;
Go home, prepare him, tell him, with what zeal
And willingness, I do it: swear it was,
On the first hearing, as thou mayst do, truly,
Mine own free motion.
MOSCA Sir, I warrant you, 95
I'll so possess him with it, that the rest
Of his starved clients shall be banished, all;
And only you received. But come not, sir,
Until I send, for I have something else
To ripen, for your good; you must not know it. 100
CORVINO
But do not you forget to send, now.
MOSCA Fear not. [*Exit* MOSCA]

75 *'Slight* God's light 75 *engaged* involved
83 *motioned* proposed
84 *make your count* count on it; or possibly 'count your gains'
85 *taking a possession* Mosca uses the legal phrase in a grotesque context
90 *wit* intelligence 90 *brief* quick
99–100 *something . . . ripen* i.e. the plot to disinherit Corbaccio's son

Act II, Scene vii

CORVINO
Where are you, wife? my Celia? wife!

[*Enter* CELIA *weeping*]

What, blubbering?
Come, dry those tears. I think, thou thought'st me in earnest?
Ha? by this light, I talked so but to try thee.
Methinks, the lightness of the occasion
Should ha'confirmed thee. Come, I am not jealous. 5

CELIA
No?

CORVINO Faith, I am not, I, nor never was:
It is a poor, unprofitable humour.
Do not I know, if women have a will,
They'll do 'gainst all the watches o' the world?
And that the fiercest spies, are tamed with gold? 10
Tut, I am confident in thee, thou shalt see't:
And see, I'll give thee cause too, to believe it.
Come, kiss me. Go, and make thee ready straight,
In all thy best attire, thy choicest jewels,
Put 'em all on, and with 'em, thy best looks: 15
We are invited to a solemn feast,
At old Volpone's, where it shall appear
How far I am free, from jealousy, or fear.

Act III, Scene i

[*A Street*]

[*Enter*] MOSCA

MOSCA
I fear, I shall begin to grow in love
With my dear self, and my most prosperous parts,
They do so spring, and burgeon; I can feel
A whimsy i' my blood: I know not how,

5 *confirmed* assured
8 *will* sexual appetite
9 *watches* watchmen, or vigilances in general
16 *solemn* formal, sumptuous
2 *parts* abilities
4 *whimsy* vertigo, whirling

Success hath made me wanton. I could skip 5
Out of my skin, now, like a subtle snake,
I am so limber. O! your parasite
Is a most precious thing, dropped from above,
Not bred 'mongst clods, and clotpoles, here on earth.
I muse the mystery was not made a science, 10
It is so liberally professed! Almost
All the wise world is little else, in nature,
But parasites, or sub-parasites. And yet,
I mean not those, that have your bare town-art,
To know, who's fit to feed 'em; have no house, 15
No family, no care, and therefore mould
Tales for men's ears, to bait that sense; or get
Kitchen-invention, and some stale receipts
To please the belly, and the groin; not those,
With their court-dog-tricks, that can fawn, and fleer, 20
Make their revènue out of legs and faces,
Echo my lord, and lick away a moth:
But your fine, elegant rascal, that can rise,
And stoop, almost together, like an arrow;
Shoot through the air, as nimbly as a star; 25
Turn short, as doth a swallow; and be here,
And there, and here, and yonder, all at once;
Present to any humour, all occasion;
And change a visor, swifter, than a thought!
This is the creature, had the art born with him; 30

6 *subtle* applied to the snake to signify its elusive movement, its texture and its traditional cunning
7 *limber* pliant, supple
10 *mystery* professional craft
10 *science* branch of formal knowledge
11 *liberally* 'widely practised by gentlemen'; Mosca puns on the sense describing the sciences 'worthy of a free man' (see *OED*)
14 *bare town-art* the minimal skills of a street parasite, described in lines 15–23
16–17 *mould Tales* concoct scandal, with suggestion of shaping traps for the ear
18 *Kitchen-invention* perhaps new ways of preparing old dishes ('stale receipts'); or possibly 'kitchen gossip'; invention need not imply novelty (see *OED*)
19 *groin* suggests that the receipts (recipes) include aphrodisiacs
20 *fleer* smile obsequiously
21 *legs and faces* bows and smirks
22 *lick . . . moth* servile grooming; 'moth' signified vermin in general
29 *visor* mask, hence 'expression' or 'role'

Toils not to learn it, but doth practise it
Out of most excellent nature: and such sparks,
Are the true parasites, others but their zanies.

Act III, Scene ii

[*Enter* BONARIO]

MOSCA
Who's this? Bonario? old Corbaccio's son?
The person I was bound to seek. Fair sir,
You are happ'ly met.

BONARIO That cannot be, by thee.

MOSCA
Why, sir?

BONARIO Nay, 'pray thee know thy way, and leave me:
I would be loath to interchange discourse, 5
With such a mate, as thou art.

MOSCA Courteous sir,
Scorn not my poverty.

BONARIO Not I, by heaven:
But thou shalt give me leave to hate thy baseness.

MOSCA
Baseness?

BONARIO Ay, answer me, is not thy sloth
Sufficient argument? thy flattery? 10
Thy means of feeding?

MOSCA Heaven, be good to me.
These imputations are too common, sir,
And eas'ly stuck on virtue, when she's poor;
You are unequal to me, and howe'er
Your sentence may be righteous, yet you are not, 15
That ere you know me, thus, proceed in censure:
St. Mark bear witness 'gainst you, 'tis inhuman. [*weeps*]

BONARIO
What? does he weep? the sign is soft, and good!
I do repent me, that I was so harsh.

MOSCA
'Tis true, that, swayed by strong necessity, 20
I am enforced to eat my careful bread

33 *zanies* attendant clowns; see II. ii, 28, 114n.
2 *bound* on my way
14 *unequal* unjust, but with allusion to the difference of station
21 *careful* hard-won

With too much obsequy; 'tis true, beside,
That I am fain to spin mine own poor raiment,
Out of my mere observance, being not born
To a free fortune: but that I have done 25
Base offices, in rending friends asunder,
Dividing families, betraying counsels,
Whispering false lies, or mining men with praises,
Trained their credulity with perjuries,
Corrupted chastity, or am in love 30
With mine own tender ease, but would not rather
Prove the most rugged, and laborious course,
That might redeem my present estimation;
Let me here perish, in all hope of goodness.

BONARIO
This cannot be a personated passion! 35
I was to blame, so to mistake thy nature;
'Pray thee forgive me: and speak out thy business.

MOSCA
Sir, it concerns you; and though I may seem,
At first, to make a main offence, in manners,
And in my gratitude, unto my master, 40
Yet, for the pure love, which I bear all right,
And hatred of the wrong, I must reveal it.
This very hour, your father is in purpose
To disinherit you—

BONARIO How!

MOSCA And thrust you forth,
As a mere stranger to his blood; 'tis true, sir: 45
The work no way engageth me, but, as
I claim an interest in the general state
Of goodness, and true virtue, which I hear
T'abound in you: and, for which mere respect,
Without a second aim, sir, I have done it. 50

BONARIO
This tale hath lost thee much of the late trust,
Thou hadst with me; it is impossible:
I know not how to lend it any thought,
My father should be so unnatural.

23 *fain* obliged
24 *observance* dutiful service
28 *mining* undermining
29 *Trained* taken in, led on (see *OED*)
32 *Prove* undergo
39 *main* major
49 *for . . . respect* for which reason alone

MOSCA
It is a confidence, that well becomes 55
Your piety; and formed, no doubt, it is,
From your own simple innocence: which makes
Your wrong more monstrous, and abhorred. But, sir,
I now, will tell you more. This very minute,
It is, or will be doing: and, if you 60
Shall be but pleased to go with me, I'll bring you,
I dare not say where you shall see, but where
Your ear shall be a witness of the deed;
Hear yourself written bastard: and professed
The common issue of the earth.

BONARIO I'm mazed! 65

MOSCA
Sir, if I do it not, draw your just sword,
And score your vengeance, on my front, and face;
Mark me your villain: you have too much wrong,
And I do suffer for you, sir. My heart
Weeps blood, in anguish—

BONARIO Lead. I follow thee. 70

Act III, Scene iii

[VOLPONE's *house*]

[*Enter* VOLPONE, *followed by* NANO, ANDROGYNO *and* CASTRONE]

VOLPONE
Mosca stays long, methinks. Bring forth your sports
And help to make the wretched time more sweet.

NANO
Dwarf, Fool, and Eunuch, well met here we be.
A question it were now, whether of us three,
Being, all, the known delicates of a rich man. 5
In pleasing him, claim the precedency can?

CASTRONE I claim for myself.

ANDROGYNO And, so doth the fool.

56 *piety* filial love (Latin *pietas*)
64 *professed* proclaimed
65 *common . . . earth* of obscure or unknown parentage (Latin *terrae filius*)
67 *score* mark up
67 *front* forehead or face
4 *whether* which 5 *known delicates* acknowledged indulgences

NANO

'Tis foolish indeed: let me set you both to school.
First, for your dwarf, he's little, and witty,
And every thing, as it is little, is pretty; 10
Else, why do men say to a creature of my shape,
So soon as they see him, 'It's a pretty little ape?'
And, why a pretty ape? but for pleasing imitation
Of greater men's action, in a ridiculous fashion.
Beside, this feat body of mind doth not crave 15
Half the meat, drink, and cloth, one of your bulks will have.
Admit, your fool's face be the mother of laughter,
Yet, for his brain, it must always come after:
And, though that do feed him, it's a pitiful case,
His body is beholding to such a bad face. 20

One knocks

VOLPONE

Who's there? my couch; away, look Nano, see:
Give me my caps, first—go, enquire!

[*Exeunt* NANO, ANDROGYNO, CASTRONE; VOLPONE *to his bed*]

Now, Cupid
Send it be Mosca, and with fair return.

NANO [*At the door*]

It is the beauteous madam—

VOLPONE Would-be—is it?

NANO

The same.

VOLPONE Now, torment on me; squire her in: 25
For she will enter, or dwell here for ever.
Nay, quickly, that my fit were past. I fear
A second hell too, that my loathing this
Will quite expel my appetite to the other:
Would she were taking, now, her tedious leave. 30
Lord, how it threats me, what I am to suffer!

15 *feat* dainty
23 *fair return* i.e. from a profitable venture

Act III, Scene iv

[*Enter* NANO *with* LADY WOULD-BE]

LADY WOULD-BE
I thank you, good sir. Pray you signify
Unto your patron, I am here. This band
Shows not my neck enough—I trouble you, sir,
Let me request you, bid one of my women
Come hither to me—in good faith, I am dressed 5
Most favourably today, it is no matter,

[*Enter* 1st WOMAN]

'Tis well enough. Look, see, these petulant things!
How they have done this!
VOLPONE I do feel the fever
Ent'ring, in at mine ears; O for a charm,
To fright it hence.
LADY WOULD-BE Come nearer: is this curl 10
In his right place? or this? why is this higher
Than all the rest? you ha'not washed your eyes, yet?
Or do they not stand even i' your head?
Where's your fellow? call her. [*Exit* 1st WOMAN]
NANO Now, St. Mark
Deliver us: anon, she'll beat her women, 15
Because her nose is red.

[*Enter* 1st WOMAN *with* 2nd WOMAN]

LADY WOULD-BE I pray you, view
This tire, forsooth: are all things apt, or no?
1st WOMAN
One hair a little, here, sticks out, forsooth.
LADY WOULD-BE
Does't so forsooth? and where was your dear sight
When it did so, forsooth? what now? bird-eyed? 20
And you, too? pray you both approach, and mend it.

2 *band* ruff or collar
6 *favourably* pleasingly (but ironic)
15 *anon* shortly
17 *tire* head-dress
20 *bird-eyed* probably 'pop-eyed', startled; possibly 'short-sighted' or 'timid'

Now, by that light, I muse, you're not ashamed!
I, that have preached these things, so oft, unto you,
Read you the principles, argued all the grounds,
Disputed every fitness, every grace, 25
Called you to counsel of so frequent dressings—

NANO [*aside*]
More carefully, than of your fame, or honour.

LADY WOULD-BE
Made you acquainted, what an ample dowry
The knowledge of these things would be unto you,
Able, alone, to get you noble husbands 30
At your return: and you, thus, to neglect it?
Besides, you seeing what a curious nation
Th'Italians are, what will they say of me?
'The English lady cannot dress herself.'—
Here's a fine imputation, to our country! 35
Well, go your ways, and stay, i'the next room.
This fucus was too coarse too, it's no matter.
Good sir, you'll give 'em entertainment?
[*Exeunt* NANO, 1st *and* 2nd WOMEN]

VOLPONE
The storm comes toward me.

LADY WOULD-BE
How does my Volp?

VOLPONE
Troubled with noise, I cannot sleep; I dreamt 40
That a strange fury entered, now, my house,
And, with the dreadful tempest of her breath,
Did cleave my roof asunder.

LADY WOULD-BE
Believe me, and I
Had the most fearful dream, could I remember 't—

VOLPONE
Out on my fate; I ha'given her the occasion 45
How to torment me: she will tell me hers.

LADY WOULD-BE
Methought, the golden mediocrity
Polite, and delicate—

VOLPONE
O, if you do love me,

23–25 *preached . . . grace* Lady Would-be deploys the terminology of formal rhetoric
27 *fame* reputation
32 *curious* particular about details
37 *fucus* cosmetic paste
47 *golden mediocrity* a travesty of the 'golden mean'

No more; I sweat, and suffer, at the mention
Of any dream: feel, how I tremble yet. 50

LADY WOULD-BE
Alas, good soul! the passion of the heart.
Seed-pearl were good now, boiled with syrup of apples,
Tincture of gold, and coral, citron-pills,
Your elecampane root, myrobalanes—

VOLPONE [*aside*]
Ay me, I have ta'en a grass-hopper by the wing. 55

LADY WOULD-BE
Burnt silk, and amber, you have muscadel
Good i' the house—

VOLPONE
You will not drink, and part?

LADY WOULD-BE
No, fear not that. I doubt, we shall not get
Some English saffron—half a dram would serve—
Your sixteen cloves, a little musk, dried mints, 60
Bugloss, and barley-meal—

VOLPONE
She's in again,
Before I feigned diseases, now I have one.

LADY WOULD-BE
And these applied, with a right scarlet cloth—

VOLPONE
Another flood of words! a very torrent!

LADY WOULD-BE
Shall I, sir, make you a poultice?

VOLPONE
No, no, no; 65
I'm very well: you need prescribe no more.

51 *passion of the heart* heartburn
52 *Seed-pearl* said by Burton to 'avail to the exhilaration of the heart' (*Anatomy of Melancholy* (1632), p. 376)
53 *coral* hung around the neck, supposed to drive away fears, devils and bad dreams
54 *elecampane* plant with bitter aromatic leaves and root, used as stimulant
54 *myrobalanes* astringent plum-like fruit prescribed for melancholy and agues
56 *Burnt silk* taken in water for the small-pox
56 *amber* used to perfume the air
59 *saffron* then grown in England (e.g. at Saffron Walden) for medical and confectory use
61 *Bugloss* recommended by Burton as a heart stimulant (*Anatomy* (1632), p. 373)
63 *scarlet cloth* another treatment for small-pox; the patient was wrapped in it

LADY WOULD-BE
I have, a little, studied physic; but, now,
I'm all for music: save, i'the forenoons,
An hour, or two, for painting. I would have
A lady, indeed, to have all, letters, and arts, 70
Be able to discourse, to write, to paint,
But principal, as Plato holds, your music,
And so does wise Pythagoras, I take it,
Is your true rapture; when there is concent
In face, in voice, and clothes: and is, indeed, 75
Our sex's chiefest ornament.

VOLPONE
The poet,
As old in time, as Plato, and as knowing,
Says that your highest female grace is silence.

LADY WOULD-BE
Which o' your poets? Petrarch? or Tasso? or Dante?
Guarini? Ariosto? Aretine? 80
Cieco di Hadria? I have read them all.

VOLPONE
Is everything a cause, to my destruction?

LADY WOULD-BE
I think, I ha' two or three of 'em, about me.

VOLPONE
The sun, the sea will sooner, both, stand still,
Than her eternal tongue! nothing can scape it. 85

68 *forenoons* mornings
74 *concent* harmony, concord
76 *The poet* i.e. Sophocles, *Ajax* 293
81 *Cieco di Hadria* 'the blind man of Adria', Luigi Groto (1541–1585), a prolific, but minor, poet in comparison with the five first named

---

67–112 In this exchange Jonson appears to be fresh from a reading of the preface to Florio's *World of Words* (1598) where Florio commends Lucie, Countess of Bedford: '[You] by conceited industrie, or industrious conceit, in Italian as in French, in French as in Spanish, in all as in English, understand what you read, write as you read, and speak as you write; yet rather charge your mind with matter than your memory with words.' Florio observes the difficulties of Italian literature: 'And I have seen the best, yea natural Italians, not only stagger, but even stick fast in the myre, and at last give it over, or give their verdict with an *ignoramus*. *Boccace* is prettie hard, yet understood: *Petrarch* harder, but explained: *Dante* hardest, but commented. Some doubt if all right.' Lady Would-be is perhaps a would-be Countess of Bedford.

LADY WOULD-BE
Here's *Pastor Fido*—
VOLPONE
Profess obstinate silence,
That's now, my safest.
LADY WOULD-BE
All our English writers,
I mean such, as are happy in th'Italian,
Will deign to steal out of this author, mainly;
Almost as much, as from Montagnié: 90
He has so modern, and facile a vein,
Fitting the time, and catching the court-ear.
Your Petrarch is more passionate, yet he,
In days of sonneting, trusted 'em, with much:
Dante is hard, and few can understand him. 95
But, for a desperate wit, there's Aretine!
Only, his pictures are a little obscene—
You mark me not?
VOLPONE
Alas, my mind's perturb'd.
LADY WOULD-BE
Why, in such cases, we must cure ourselves,
Make use of our philosophy—
VOLPONE
O'y me! 100
LADY WOULD-BE
And, as we find our passions do rebel,
Encounter 'em with reason; or divert 'em,
By giving scope unto some other humour
Of lesser danger: as, in politic bodies,
There's nothing, more, doth overwhelm the judgement, 105
And clouds the understanding, than too much
Settling, and fixing, and (as't were) subsiding
Upon one object. For the incorporating
Of these same outward things, into that part,

86 *Pastor Fido* Guarini's pastoral (1590), translated into English as *The Faithful Shepherd* in 1602
90 *Montagnié* Q (F Montagnie); the Q accent suggests four syllables in pronunciation
94 *trusted . . . much* left much in their keeping; Petrarch was imitated as a sonneteer by Wyatt, Surrey, Sidney and Spenser, among others
96 *desperate wit* outrageous poet; Aretino wrote a number of pornographic poems including the sixteen *Sonnetti lussoriosi* which were published to designs by Giulio Romano in 1523
104 *politic bodies* kingdoms, states
105–112 *overwhelm . . . knowledge* Lady Would-be's theories of obsession and perception are a travesty of Platonic thinking

Which we call mental, leaves some certain faeces 110
That stop the organs, and, as Plato says,
Assassinates our knowledge.

VOLPONE Now, the spirit
Of patience help me.

LADY WOULD-BE Come, in faith, I must
Visit you more a days; and make you well:
Laugh, and be lusty.

VOLPONE My good angel save me! 115

LADY WOULD-BE
There was but one sole man, in all the world,
With whom I ere could sympathize; and he
Would lie you often, three, four hours together,
To hear me speak: and be, sometime, so rapt,
As he would answer me, quite from the purpose, 120
Like you, and you are like him, just. I'll discourse,
And't be but only, sir, to bring you asleep,
How we did spend our time, and loves, together,
For some six years.

VOLPONE Oh, oh, oh, oh, oh, oh.

LADY WOULD-BE
For we were *coætanei*, and brought up— 125

VOLPONE [*aside*]
Some power, some fate, some fortune rescue me!

Act III, Scene v

[*Enter* MOSCA]

MOSCA
God save you, madam!

LADY WOULD-BE Good sir.

VOLPONE Mosca! welcome,
Welcome to my redemption!

MOSCA Why, sir?

VOLPONE Oh,
Rid me of this my torture, quickly, there;
My Madam, with the everlasting voice:
The bells, in time of pestilence, ne'er made 5
Like noise, or were in that perpetual motion;

114 *more a days* on more days, more often (compare 'nowadays')
125 *coætanei* of the same age (*co-aetaneus*)
5 *bells . . . pestilence* death knells; see F. P. Wilson, *The Plague in Shakespeare's London* (1927) p. 177, equally relevant to Venice

The cock-pit comes not near it. All my house,
But now, steamed like a bath, with her thick breath.
A lawyer could not have been heard; nor scarce
Another woman, such a hail of words 10
She has let fall. For hell's sake, rid her hence.

MOSCA
Has she presented?

VOLPONE O, I do not care,
I'll take her absence, upon any price,
With any loss.

MOSCA Madam—

LADY WOULD-BE I ha'brought your patron
A toy, a cap here, of mine own work—

MOSCA 'Tis well, 15
I had forgot to tell you, I saw your knight,
Where you'd little think it—

LADY WOULD-BE Where?

MOSCA Marry,
Where yet, if you make haste, you may apprehend him,
Rowing upon the water in a gondola,
With the most cunning courtesan of Venice. 20

LADY WOULD-BE
Is't true?

MOSCA Pursue 'em, and believe your eyes:
Leave me, to make your gift. [*Exit* LADY WOULD-BE] I knew 'twould take.
For lightly, they that use themselves most licence,
Are still most jealous.

VOLPONE Mosca, hearty thanks,
For thy quick fiction, and delivery of me. 25
Now, to my hopes, what say'st thou?

[*Enter* LADY WOULD-BE]

LADY WOULD-BE But do you hear, sir?—

VOLPONE
Again; I fear a paroxysm.

LADY WOULD-BE Which way
Rowed they together?

MOSCA Toward the Rialto.

7 *cock-pit* to be found in Venice or London; the Drury lane cock-pit was enclosed and later became a theatre; see Hogarth's print of the cock-pit in Birdcage Walk.
23 *lightly* often, usually
24 *still* always

LADY WOULD-BE
I pray you lend me your dwarf.

MOSCA
I pray you, take him.
[*Exit* LADY WOULD-BE]

Your hopes, sir, are like happy blossoms, fair, 30
And promise timely fruit, if you will stay
But the maturing; keep you, at your couch,
Corbaccio will arrive straight, with the will:
When he is gone, I'll tell you more.

VOLPONE
My blood,
My spirits are returned; I am alive: 35
And like your wanton gamester, at *primero*,
Whose thought had whispered to him, not go less,
Methinks I lie, and draw—for an encounter

[VOLPONE *draws the curtains across his bed*]

Act III, Scene vi

[MOSCA *leads* BONARIO *in and hides him*]

MOSCA
Sir, here concealed, you may hear all. But pray you
Have patience, sir; (*One knocks*) the same's your father, knocks:
I am compelled to leave you.

BONARIO
Do so. Yet,
Cannot my thought imagine this a truth.

Act III, Scene vii

[MOSCA *admits* CORVINO *and* CELIA]

MOSCA
Death on me! you are come too soon, what meant you?
Did not I say, I would send?

CORVINO
Yes, but I feared
You might forget it, and then they prevent us.

MOSCA
Prevent? [*aside*]—Did e'er man haste so, for his horns?
A courtier would not ply it so, for a place.— 5

36 *primero* a gambling card-game resembling poker; Volpone puns on its technical terms 'go less', 'lie', 'draw' and 'encounter'
s.d. For the staging of this and subsequent scenes see p. xxix
2 *Did . . . send* see II. vi, 99

Well, now there's no helping it, stay here;
I'll presently return. [*Moves toward* BONARIO]

CORVINO Where are you, Celia?
You know not wherefore I have brought you hither?

CELIA
Not well, except you told me.

CORVINO Now, I will:
Hark hither. [*They converse apart*]

MOSCA (*To* BONARIO) Sir, your father hath sent word, 10
It will be half an hour, ere he come;
And therefore, if you please to walk, the while,
Into that gallery—at the upper end,
There are some books to entertain the time:
And I'll take care, no man shall come unto you, sir. 15

BONARIO
Yes, I will stay there. [*Aside*] I do doubt this fellow.
[*Exit* BONARIO *to the gallery*]

MOSCA
There, he is far enough; he can hear nothing:
And, for his father, I can keep him off. [*Moves to* VOLPONE]

CORVINO
Nay, now, there is no starting back; and therefore,
Resolve upon it: I have so decreed. 20
It must be done. Nor, would I move't afore,
Because I would avoid all shifts and tricks,
That might deny me.

CELIA Sir, let me beseech you,
Affect not these strange trials; if you doubt
My chastity, why lock me up, for ever: 25
Make me the heir of darkness. Let me live,
Where I may please your fears, if not your trust.

CORVINO
Believe it, I have no such humour, I.
All that I speak, I mean; yet I am not mad:
Not horn-mad, see you? Go to, show yourself 30
Obedient, and a wife.

CELIA O heaven!

9 *except* except what
21 *move* urge
24 *Affect* seek (not necessarily implying pretence)
24 *strange* exceptional, extreme
30 *horn-mad* mad at being cuckolded, mad at the prospect, or mad to be so

CORVINO I say it,
Do so.

CELIA Was this the train?

CORVINO I've told you reasons;
What the physicians have set down; how much,
It may concern me; what my engagements are;
My means; and the necessity of those means, 35
For my recovery: wherefore, if you be
Loyal, and mine, be won, respect my venture.

CELIA
Before your honour?

CORVINO Honour? tut, a breath;
There's no such thing, in nature: a mere term
Invented to awe fools. What is my gold 40
The worse, for touching? clothes for being looked on?
Why, this's no more. An old, decrepit wretch,
That has no sense, no sinew; takes his meat
With others' fingers; only knows to gape,
When you do scald his gums; a voice; a shadow; 45
And what can this man hurt you?

CELIA Lord! what spirit
Is this hath entered him?

CORVINO And for your fame,
That's such a jig; as if I would go tell it,
Cry it, on the Piazza! who shall know it?
But he, that cannot speak it; and this fellow, 50
Whose lips are i' my pocket: save yourself,
If you'll proclaim't, you may. I know no other,
Should come to know it.

CELIA Are heaven, and saints then nothing?
Will they be blind, or stupid?

CORVINO How?

CELIA Good sir,
Be jealous still, emulate them; and think 55
What hate they burn with, toward every sin.

CORVINO
I grant you: if I thought it were a sin,
I would not urge you. Should I offer this
To some young Frenchman, or hot Tuscan blood,
That had read Aretine, conned all his prints, 60

32 *train* trick, trap (see III. ii, 29)
35 *means* financial resources 37 *venture* enterprise
43 *sense* sensory awareness
48 *jig* trifle 60 *prints* see III. iv, 96n.

Knew every quirk within lust's labyrinth,
And were professed critic, in lechery:
And I would look upon him, and applaud him,
This were a sin: but here, 'tis contrary,
A pious work, mere charity, for physic, 65
And honest polity, to assure mine own.

CELIA
O heaven! canst thou suffer such a change?

VOLPONE
Thou art mine honour, Mosca, and my pride,
My joy, my tickling, my delight! go, bring 'em.

MOSCA
Please you draw near, sir.

CORVINO Come on, what— 70
You will not be rebellious? by that light—
[*Drags her to the bed*]
Sir, Signior Corvino, here, is come to see you—

VOLPONE
Oh!

MOSCA And hearing of the consultation had,
So lately, for your health, is come to offer,
Or rather, sir, to prostitute—

CORVINO Thanks, sweet Mosca. 75

MOSCA
Freely, unasked, or unentreated—

CORVINO Well.

MOSCA
As the true, fervent instance of his love,
His own most fair and proper wife; the beauty,
Only of price, in Venice—

CORVINO 'Tis well urged.

MOSCA
To be your comfortress, and to preserve you. 80

VOLPONE
Alas, I'm past already! pray you, thank him,
For his good care, and promptness, but for that,
'Tis a vain labour, e'en to fight 'gainst heaven;
Applying fire to a stone: —uh, uh, uh, uh.—
Making a dead leaf grow again. I take 85

61 *quirk* sudden twist
62 *professed critic* qualified expert
63 *And* if
66 *mine own* i.e. the inheritance
79 *Only of price* of unique excellence

His wishes gently, though; and, you may tell him,
What I've done for him: marry, my state is hopeless!
Will him, to pray for me; and t'use his fortune,
With reverence, when he comes to't.

MOSCA
Do you hear, sir?
Go to him, with your wife.

CORVINO
Heart of my father! 90
Wilt thou persist thus? come, I pray thee, come.
Thou seest 'tis nothing: Celia! by this hand
I shall grow violent. Come, do't, I say.

CELIA
Sir, kill me, rather: I will take down poison,
Eat burning coals, do anything—

CORVINO
Be damned! 95
Heart, I will drag thee hence, home, by the hair;
Cry thee a strumpet, through the streets; rip up
Thy mouth, unto thine ears; and slit thy nose,
Like a raw rotchet—Do not tempt me, come.
Yield, I am loath—Death, I will buy some slave, 100
Whom I will kill, and bind thee to him, alive;
And at my window, hang you forth: devising
Some monstrous crime, which I, in capital letters,
Will eat into thy flesh, with aquafortis,
And burning corsives, on this stubborn breast. 105
Now, by the blood, thou hast incensed, I'll do't.

CELIA
Sir, what you please, you may; I am your martyr.

CORVINO
Be not thus obstinate, I ha' not deserved it:
Think, who it is, entreats you. Pray thee, sweet;
Good faith, thou shalt have jewels, gowns, attires, 110
What thou wilt think, and ask—Do, but, go kiss him.
Or touch him, but. For my sake. At my suit.
This once. No? not? I shall remember this.
Will you disgrace me, thus? do you thirst my undoing?

MOSCA
Nay, gentle lady, be advised.

CORVINO
No, no. 115

95 *Eat . . . coals* Brutus's wife, Portia, died in this way
99 *rotchet* the red gurnet
100 *some slave* this was Tarquin's threat to Lucrece; see *Rape of Lucrece* 515, 671
104 *aquafortis* nitric acid, used for etching
105 *corsives* corrosives

She has watched her time. God's precious, this is scurvy;
'Tis very scurvy: and you are—.

MOSCA
Nay, good sir.

CORVINO
An errant locust, by heaven, a locust. Whore,
Crocodile, that hast thy tears prepared,
Expecting, how thou'lt bid 'em flow.

MOSCA
Nay, pray you, sir, 120
She will consider.

CELIA
Would my life would serve
To satisfy—

CORVINO
'Sdeath, if she would but speak to him,
And save my reputation, 'twere somewhat;
But, spitefully to affect my utter ruin—

MOSCA
Ay, now you've put your fortune in her hands. 125
Why i'faith, it is her modesty, I must quit her;
If you were absent, she would be more coming;
I know it: and dare undertake for her.
What woman can, before her husband? Pray you,
Let us depart, and leave her, here.

CORVINO
Sweet Celia, 130
Thou mayst redeem all, yet; I'll say no more:
If not, esteem yourself as lost. [CELIA *starts to leave*]. Nay,
stay there. [*Exeunt* CORVINO, MOSCA]

CELIA
O God, and his good angels! whither, whither
Is shame fled human breasts? that with such ease,
Men dare put off your honours, and their own? 135
Is that, which ever was a cause of life,
Now placed beneath the basest circumstance?
And modesty an exile made, for money?

VOLPONE
Ay, in Corvino, and such earth-fed minds,
He leaps off from his couch
That never tasted the true heaven of love. 140

116 *God's precious* i.e. precious blood
118 *errant* either 'wandering' or 'arrant, downright'; the senses are related and both applicable—'arrant, promiscuous parasite'
119 *Crocodile* believed to entice its victims with artful tears
120 *Expecting* anticipating
124 *ruin*— (F ruin. Q ruin:) Q indicates that the thought is incomplete, or that Mosca interrupts it; some editors read 'ruin!'
126 *quit* clear, acquit 127 *coming* forthcoming, responsive

Assure thee, Celia, he that would sell thee,
Only for hope of gain, and that uncertain,
He would have sold his part of paradise
For ready money, had he met a cope-man.
Why art thou mazed, to see me thus revived? 145
Rather applaud thy beauty's miracle;
'Tis thy great work: that hath, not now alone,
But sundry times, raised me, in several shapes,
And, but this morning, like a mountebank,
To see thee at thy window. Ay, before 150
I would have left my practice, for thy love,
In varying figures, I would have contended
With the blue Proteus, or the hornèd flood.
Now, art thou welcome.

CELIA Sir!

VOLPONE Nay, fly me not.

Nor, let thy false imagination 155
That I was bedrid, make thee think, I am so:
Thou shalt not find it. I am, now, as fresh,
As hot, as high, and in as jovial plight,
As when, in that so celebrated scene,
At recitation of our comedy, 160
For entertainment of the great Valois,
I acted young Antinous; and attracted
The eyes, and ears of all the ladies present,
T'admire each graceful gesture, note, and footing.

Song 165

Come, my Celia, let us prove,
While we can, the sports of love;

144 *cope-man* chapman, dealer 145 *mazed* bewildered
151 *practice* scheming, intriguing
152 *figures* appearances, shapes
153 *blue Proteus* marine blue (Latin *caeruleus*); Menelaus contends with the many shapes of Proteus (*Odyssey* IV. 456–458)
153 *hornèd flood* the river-god Achelous who fought Hercules in the forms of bull, serpent, and man-bull; the shape may symbolise the river's branchings and its roar
158 *jovial* born under Jupiter, and therefore apt to share Jove's convivial temperament and amorous propensities
158 *plight* state, trim
161 *Valois* Henry of Valois was entertained at Venice in 1574
162 *Antinous* beautiful youth, minion of the Emperor Hadrian
165 *Song* imitated largely from Catullus's fifth ode, *Vivamus, mea Lesbia* (see pp. xv, xxx) 166 *prove* try

Time will not be ours, for ever,
He, at length, our good will sever;
Spend not then his gifts, in vain. 170
Suns, that set, may rise again:
But if, once, we lose this light,
'Tis with us perpetual night.
Why should we defer our joys?
Fame, and rumour are but toys. 175
Cannot we delude the eyes
Of a few poor household spies?
Or his easier ears beguile,
Thus removèd, by our wile?
'Tis no sin, love's fruits to steal; 180
But the sweet thefts to reveal:
To be taken, to be seen,
These have crimes accounted been.

CELIA
Some *serene* blast me, or dire lightning strike
This my offending face.

VOLPONE Why droops my Celia? 185
Thou hast in place of a base husband, found
A worthy lover: use thy fortune well,
With secrecy, and pleasure. See, behold,
What thou art queen of; not in expectation,
As I feed others; but possessed, and crowned. 190
See, here, a rope of pearl; and each, more orient
Than that the brave Egyptian queen caroused:
Dissolve, and drink 'em. See, a carbuncle,
May put out both the eyes of our St. Mark;
A diamant, would have bought Lollia Paulina, 195

175 *toys* trifles
184 *serene* (French *serein*) twilight mist in hot countries; once thought noxious 191 *orient* rare and fine (see I. v, 9)
192 *Egyptian queen* Pliny (*Naturalis Historia* IX.120) tells how Cleopatra met Antony's challenge to spend a hundred hundred thousand sesterces at a meal by drinking a priceless pearl dissolved in vinegar
194 *both . . . St. Mark* perhaps an image of St. Mark with gems for eyes, but none is recorded; possibly two famous carbuncles in Venice, one in St. Mark's treasury; possibly an extravagant sacrilegious metaphor; see p. 164
195 *Lollia Paulina* wife of the Emperor Caligula; an heiress whose wealth was extorted from the provinces by her father; Pliny describes her clad in jewels and glittering like the sun at a betrothal party; see Introduction p. xxiv

When she came in, like star-light, hid with jewels,
That were the spoils of provinces; take these,
And wear, and lose 'em: yet remains an ear-ring
To purchase them again, and this whole state.
A gem, but worth a private patrimony, 200
Is nothing: we will eat such at a meal.
The heads of parrots, tongues of nightingales,
The brains of peacocks, and of ostriches
Shall be our food: and, could we get the phoenix,
Though nature lost her kind, she were our dish. 205

CELIA
Good sir, these things might move a mind affected
With such delights; but I, whose innocence
Is all I can think wealthy, or worth th'enjoying,
And which once lost, I have nought to lose beyond it,
Cannot be taken with these sensual baits: 210
If you have conscience—

VOLPONE 'Tis the beggar's virtue,
If thou hast wisdom, hear me, Celia.
Thy baths shall be the juice of July-flowers,
Spirit of roses, and of violets,
The milk of unicorns, and panthers' breath 215
Gathered in bags, and mixed with Cretan wines.
Our drink shall be preparèd gold, and amber;
Which we will take, until my roof whirl round
With the vertigo: and my dwarf shall dance,
My eunuch sing, my fool make up the antic. 220
Whilst we, in changèd shapes, act Ovid's tales,
Thou, like Europa now, and I like Jove,
Then I like Mars, and thou like Erycine,
So, of the rest, till we have quite run through

204 *phoenix* the mythical Arabian bird, supposed to renew itself from its own ashes every five hundred years
213 *July-flowers* gillyflowers (clove-scented pinks)
215 *milk of unicorns* a delicacy found only here; but powdered unicorn horn (from the rhinoceros) was used as medicine
215 *panthers' breath* panthers were said to attract their prey by the sweetness of their scent
216 *Cretan wines* rather rich and sweet for bathing (see I. i, 58); there is evidence that Mary Queen of Scots habitually bathed in wine
220 *antic* grotesque dance
221 *Ovid's tales* i.e. *Metamorphoses*
222 *Europa . . . Jove* Zeus won Europa by playing with her in the form of a bull before bearing her to Crete on his back
223 *Erycine* Venus, after her temple at Eryx in Sicily

And wearied all the fables of the gods. 225
Then will I have thee in more modern forms,
Attired like some sprightly dame of France,
Brave Tuscan lady, or proud Spanish beauty;
Sometimes, unto the Persian Sophy's wife;
Or the Grand Signor's mistress; and, for change, 230
To one of our most artful courtesans,
Or some quick Negro, or cold Russian;
And I will meet thee, in as many shapes:
Where we may, so, transfuse our wand'ring souls,
Out at our lips, and score up sums of pleasures, [*Sings*] 235
That the curious shall not know,
How to tell them, as they flow;
And the envious, when they find
What their number is, be pined.

CELIA

If you have ears that will be pierced; or eyes, 240
That can be opened; a heart, may be touched;
Or any part, that yet sounds man, about you:
If you have touch of holy saints, or heaven,
Do me the grace, to let me scape. If not,
Be bountiful, and kill me. You do know, 245
I am a creature, hither ill betrayed,
By one, whose shame I would forget it were.
If you will deign me neither of these graces,
Yet feed your wrath, sir, rather than your lust;
(It is a vice, comes nearer manliness) 250
And punish that unhappy crime of nature,
Which you miscall my beauty: flay my face,
Or poison it, with ointments, for seducing
Your blood to this rebellion. Rub these hands,
With what may cause an eating leprosy, 255
E'en to my bones, and marrow: anything,
That may disfavour me, save in my honour.

229 *Sophy* the Shah, supreme ruler
230 *Grand Signor* Sultan of Turkey
232 *quick* lively
234 *transfuse* 'to cause to flow from one to another' (*OED*); the image is from Petronius, *Satyricon* 79
239 *pined* tormented
240–260 For the Quarto punctuation of this speech see p. 169
242 *sounds man* proclaims you a man; see Introduction p. xiii, for discussion of 'virtue'
257 *disfavour* disfigure

And I will kneel to you, pray for you, pay down
A thousand hourly vows, sir, for your health,
Report, and think you virtuous—

VOLPONE
Think me cold, 260
Frozen, and impotent, and so report me?
That I had Nestor's hernia, thou wouldst think.
I do degenerate, and abuse my nation,
To play with opportunity, thus long:
I should have done the act, and then have parleyed. 265
Yield, or I'll force thee.

CELIA
O! just God.

VOLPONE
In vain—

[BONARIO] *leaps out from where Mosca had placed him*

BONARIO
Forbear, foul ravisher, libidinous swine,
Free the forced lady, or thou diest, impostor.
But that I am loath to snatch thy punishment
Out of the hand of justice, thou shouldst, yet, 270
Be made the timely sacrifice of vengeance,
Before this altar, and this dross, thy idol.
Lady, let's quit the place, it is the den
Of villainy; fear nought, you have a guard:
And he, ere long, shall meet his just reward. 275

VOLPONE
Fall on me, roof, and bury me in ruin,
Become my grave, that wert my shelter. O!
I am unmasked, unspirited, undone,
Betrayed to beggary, to infamy—

Act III, Scene viii

[*Enter* MOSCA, *bleeding*]

MOSCA
Where shall I run, most wretched shame of men,
To beat out my unlucky brains?

262 *Nestor's hernia* Nestor embodies the strengths as well as the weaknesses of age in Homer's *Iliad;* this glance at his impotence is from Juvenal, *Satires* VI, 326

263 *degenerate* possibly used transitively 'cause my nation (Italy) to lose its ancestral virtue', but the intransitive use is more probable

272 *dross* 'the scum thrown off from metals in smelting' (*OED*); a perverse dismissal of Volpone's gold

VOLPONE
Here, here.
What! dost thou bleed?

MOSCA
O, that his well-driven sword
Had been so courteous to have cleft me down,
Unto the navel; ere I lived to see 5
My life, my hopes, my spirits, my patron, all
Thus desperately engagèd, by my error.

VOLPONE
Woe, on thy fortune.

MOSCA
And my follies, sir.

VOLPONE
Th'hast made me miserable.

MOSCA
And myself, sir.
Who would have thought, he would have hearkened, so? 10

VOLPONE
What shall we do?

MOSCA
I know not, if my heart
Could expiate the mischance, I'd pluck it out.
Will you be pleased to hang me? or cut my throat?
And I'll requite you, sir. Let's die like Romans,
Since we have lived, like Grecians. *They knock without*

VOLPONE
Hark, who's there? 15
I hear some footing, officers, the Saffi
Come to apprehend us! I do feel the brand
Hissing already, at my forehead: now,
Mine ears are boring.

MOSCA
To your couch, sir, you
Make that place good, however. Guilty men 20
Suspect, what they deserve still. Signior Corbaccio!

7 *engagèd* entangled
14 *like Romans* Stoically, by suicide
15 *like Grecians* dissolutely and histrionically (see Juvenal, *Satires* III. 100ff.)
16 *footing* footsteps
16 *Saffi* '*Saffo*, a catchpole, or sergeant' (Florio 1598); bailiffs
17 *brand* Jonson himself was branded on the thumb for killing Gabriel Spencer (see p. vii)
19 *boring* this suggests ear-rings or ear-brandings for criminals, but no other evidence has been brought to bear
20 *Make . . . however* 'keep up that role whatever you do'

LX 23

Act III, Scene ix

[*Enter* CORBACCIO]

CORBACCIO
Why! how now? Mosca!

[*Enter* VOLTORE *unseen*]

MOSCA O, undone, amazed, sir.
Your son, I know not by what accident,
Acquainted with your purpose to my patron,
Touching your will, and making him your heir;
Entered our house with violence, his sword drawn, 5
Sought for you, called you wretch, unnatural,
Vowed he would kill you.

CORBACCIO Me?

MOSCA Yes, and my patron.

CORBACCIO
This act, shall disinherit him indeed:
Here is the will.

MOSCA 'Tis well, sir.

CORBACCIO Right and well.
Be you as careful now, for me.

MOSCA My life, sir, 10
Is not more tendered, I am only yours.

CORBACCIO
How does he? will he die shortly, thinkst thou?

MOSCA I fear
He'll outlast May.

CORBACCIO Today?

MOSCA No, last out May, sir.

CORBACCIO
Couldst thou not gi'him a dram?

MOSCA O, by no means, sir.

CORBACCIO
Nay, I'll not bid you.

VOLTORE [*Aside*] This is a knave, I see. 15

MOSCA [*Aside*]
How! Signior Voltore! did he hear me?

VOLTORE Parasite!

1 *amazed* confused
8 *disinherit . . . indeed* i.e. permanently
10 *careful* solicitous
11 *tendered* tenderly cared for
14 *dram* dose

MOSCA
Who's that? O, sir, most timely welcome—

VOLTORE
Scarce,
To the discovery of your tricks, I fear.
You are his, only? and mine, also? are you not?

MOSCA
Who? I, sir!

VOLTORE
You, sir. What device is this 20
About a will?

MOSCA
A plot for you, sir.

VOLTORE
Come,
Put not your foists upon me, I shall scent 'em.

MOSCA
Did you not hear it?

VOLTORE
Yes, I hear, Corbaccio
Hath made your patron, there, his heir.

MOSCA
'Tis true,
By my device, drawn to it by my plot, 25
With hope—

VOLTORE
Your patron should reciprocate?
And, you have promised?

MOSCA
For your good, I did, sir.
Nay more, I told his son, brought, hid him here,
Where he might hear his father pass the deed;
Being persuaded to it, by this thought, sir, 30
That the unnaturalness, first, of the act,
And then, his father's oft disclaiming in him,
Which I did mean t'help on, would sure enrage him
To do some violence upon his parent.
On which the law should take sufficient hold, 35
And you be stated in a double hope:
Truth be my comfort, and my conscience,
My only aim was, to dig you a fortune
Out of these two, old rotten sepulchres—

VOLTORE
I cry thee mercy, Mosca.

MOSCA
Worth your patience, 40
And your great merit, sir. And, see the change!

VOLTORE
Why? what success?

20 *device* contrivance
22 *foists* rogueries; also foist, 'to smell or grow musty' (*OED*)
32 *disclaiming in him* disowning; renouncing legal claim
36 *stated* instated
42 *success* outcome

MOSCA Most hapless! you must help, sir.
Whilst we expected th'old raven, in comes
Corvino's wife, sent hither, by her husband—

VOLTORE
What, with a present?

MOSCA No, sir, on visitation: 45
(I'll tell you how, anon) and, staying long,
The youth, he grows impatient, rushes forth,
Seizeth the lady, wounds me, makes me swear
(Or he would murder her, that was his vow)
T'affirm my patron to have done her rape: 50
Which how unlike it is, you see! and, hence,
With that pretext, he's gone, t'accuse his father;
Defame my patron; defeat you—

VOLTORE Where's her husband?
Let him be sent for, straight.

MOSCA Sir, I'll go fetch him.

VOLTORE
Bring him, to the Scrutineo.

MOSCA Sir, I will. 55

VOLTORE
This must be stopped.

MOSCA O, you do nobly, sir.
Alas, 'twas laboured all, sir, for your good;
Nor, was there any want of counsel, in the plot:
But fortune can, at any time, o'erthrow
The projects of a hundred learned clerks, sir. 60

CORBACCIO
What's that?

VOLTORE Wilt please you sir, to go along?
[*Exeunt* CORBACCIO, VOLTORE]

MOSCA
Patron, go in, and pray for our success.

VOLPONE
Need makes devotion: heaven your labour bless.

LX
23.5

42 *hapless* unfortunate
50 *to have* F (Q would have)
55 *Scrutineo* law court in Senate House
60 *clerks* scholars

Act IV, Scene i

[*A Street*]

[*Enter* SIR POLITIC WOULD-BE, PEREGRINE]

SIR POLITIC
I told you, sir, it was a plot: you see
What observation is. You mentioned me,
For some instructions: I will tell you, sir,
Since we are met, here, in this height of Venice,
Some few particulars, I have set down, 5
Only for this meridian; fit to be known
Of your crude traveller, and they are these.
I will not touch, sir, at your phrase, or clothes,
For they are old.

PEREGRINE Sir, I have better.

SIR POLITIC Pardon,
I meant, as they are themes.

PEREGRINE O, sir, proceed: 10
I'll slander you no more of wit, good sir.

SIR POLITIC
First, for your garb, it must be grave, and serious;
Very reserved, and locked; not tell a secret,
On any terms, not to your father; scarce
A fable, but with caution; make sure choice 15
Both of your company, and discourse; beware,
You never speak a truth—

PEREGRINE How!

SIR POLITIC Not to strangers,
For those be they you must converse with, most;
Others I would not know, sir, but at distance,

1 *it was a plot* i.e. the mountebank scene
2 *mentioned me* asked me in passing (?); Sir Politic resumes this false presumption from II. i, 120
4 *height* latitude
8 *your* the impersonal, familiar use which Peregrine affects to misinterpret
8 *phrase* manner of speaking
10 *themes* topics
11 *slander . . . wit* either 'I'll no more misrepresent you for the sake of being witty', or 'I'll no more accuse you of being quick-witted'
12 *garb* demeanour
15 *fable* fiction
19 *know* acknowledge

So as I still might be a saver, in 'em: 20
You shall have tricks, else, passed upon you hourly.
And then, for your religion, profess none;
But wonder, at the diversity of all;
And, for your part, protest, were there no other
But simply the laws o'the land, you could content you: 25
Nick Machiavel, and Monsieur Bodin, both,
Were of this mind. Then, must you learn the use,
And handling of your silver fork, at meals;
The metal of your glass—these are main matters,
With your Italian—and to know the hour, 30
When you must eat your melons, and your figs.

PEREGRINE
Is that a point of state, too?

SIR POLITIC
Here it is.
For your Venetian, if he see a man
Preposterous, in the least, he has him straight;
He has: he strips him. I'll acquaint you, sir, 35
I now have lived here, 'tis some fourteen months,
Within the first week of my landing here,
All took me for a citizen of Venice:
I knew the forms so well—

PEREGRINE [*Aside*]
And nothing else.

SIR POLITIC
I had read Contarene, took me a house, 40
Dealt with my Jews, to furnish it with moveables—
Well, if I could but find one man–one man,
To mine own heart– whom I durst trust, I would—

20 *be . . . 'em* 'keep myself safe in respect to them' (either from danger or from inconvenience)
26 *Machiavel . . . Bodin* the sentiments are falsely attributed, but Machiavelli did tend to subordinate religion to the state, and Jean Bodin elaborated a theory of toleration
28 *fork* forks were not much used in England at this time (see *The Devil is an Ass* V. iv, 18)
29 *metal* 'the material used for making glass, in a molten state' (*OED*); Sir Politic is exhibiting his technical knowledge
29 *main* of primary importance
34 *Preposterous* back-to-front, in the wrong order
34 *has him straight* sums him up instantly
40 *Contarene* Cardinal Gasparo Contarini published a book on Venice, *De Magistratibus et Republica Venetorum* (1589), translated into English in 1599
41 *moveables* at this time commonly distinguished from fixed furnishings

PEREGRINE
What? what, sir?
SIR POLITIC Make him rich; make him a fortune:
He should not think, again. I would command it. 45
PEREGRINE
As how?
SIR POLITIC With certain projects, that I have,
Which, I may not discover.
PEREGRINE [*Aside*] If I had
But one to wager with, I would lay odds, now,
He tells me, instantly.
SIR POLITIC One is (and that
I care not greatly, who knows) to serve the state 50
Of Venice, with red herrings, for three years,
And at a certain rate, from Rotterdam,
Where I have correspondence. There's a letter,
Sent me from one o' the States, and to that purpose;
He cannot write his name, but that's his mark. 55
PEREGRINE
He is a chandler?
SIR POLITIC No, a cheesemonger.
There are some other too, with whom I treat,
About the same negotiation;
And, I will undertake it: for, 'tis thus,
I'll do 't with ease, I've cast it all. Your hoy 60
Carries but three men in her, and a boy;
And she shall make me three returns, a year:
So, if there come but one of three, I save,
If two, I can defalk. But, this is now,
If my main project fail.
PEREGRINE Then, you have others? 65
SIR POLITIC
I should be loath to draw the subtle air
Of such a place, without my thousand aims.
I'll not dissemble, sir, where'er I come

47 *discover* reveal
53 *correspondence* connections
54 *one o'the States* a member of the Dutch assembly, the States-General
56 *chandler?* Peregrine speculates from the greasy state of the letter
60 *cast* reckoned
60 *hoy* Dutch coastal vessel, meant for short hauls
64 *defalk* allow a deduction, perhaps on the price of the herrings, but the financial strategy is obscure
66 *subtle air* atmosphere of intrigue

I love to be considerative; and, 'tis true,
I have, at my free hours, thought upon 70
Some certain goods, unto the state of Venice,
Which I do call my cautions: and, sir, which
I mean, in hope of pension, to propound
To the Great Council, then unto the Forty,
So to the Ten. My means are made already— 75

PEREGRINE
By whom?

SIR POLITIC Sir, one, that though his place be obscure,
Yet, he can sway, and they will hear him. He's
A *commendatore*.

PEREGRINE What, a common sergeant?

SIR POLITIC
Sir, such as they are, put it in their mouths,
What they should say, sometimes: as well as greater. 80
I think I have my notes, to show you—

PEREGRINE Good, sir.

SIR POLITIC
But, you shall swear unto me, on your gentry,
Not to anticipate—

PEREGRINE I, sir?

SIR POLITIC Nor reveal
A circumstance—My paper is not with me.

PEREGRINE
O, but, you can remember, sir.

SIR POLITIC My first is, 85
Concerning tinder-boxes. You must know,
No family is, here, without its box.
Now sir, it being so portable a thing,
Put case, that you, or I were ill affected
Unto the state; sir, with it in our pockets, 90
Might not I go into the *arsenale*?
Or you? come out again? and none the wiser?

69 *considerative* prudently deliberate
72 *cautions* can mean 'precautions', but taken here 'in hope of pension'
74–75 *Great . . . Ten* the administrative hierarchy of Venice
75 *means* means of access, contacts
78 *sergeant* officer charged with the arrest or summoning of offenders
79 *their mouths* i.e. the mouths of the great
89 *Put case* 'say for example'
91 *arsenale* Sir Politic may use the Italian pronunciation; the Arsenal of Venice housed all its ships and weapons

PEREGRINE
Except yourself, sir.
SIR POLITIC Go to, then. I, therefore,
Advertise to the state, how fit it were,
That none, but such as were known patriots, 95
Sound lovers of their country, should be suffered
T'enjoy them in their houses: and, even those,
Sealed, at some office, and, at such a bigness,
As might not lurk in pockets.
PEREGRINE Admirable!
SIR POLITIC
My next is, how t'enquire, and be resolved, 100
By present demonstration, whether a ship,
Newly arrived from Soria, or from
Any suspected part of all the Levant,
Be guilty of the plague: and, where they use,
To lie out forty, fifty days, sometimes, 105
About the Lazaretto, for their trial;
I'll save that charge, and loss unto the merchant,
And, in an hour, clear the doubt.
PEREGRINE Indeed, sir?
SIR POLITIC
Or—I will lose my labour.
PEREGRINE My faith, that's much.
SIR POLITIC
Nay, sir, conceive me. 'Twill cost me, in onions, 110
Some thirty *livres*—
PEREGRINE Which is one pound sterling.
SIR POLITIC
Beside my water-works: for this I do, sir.
First, I bring in your ship, 'twixt two brick walls;
(But those the state shall venture) on the one
I strain me a fair tarpaulin; and, in that, 115

94 *Advertise* make known
98 *Sealed* registered under seal
101 *present demonstration* on-the-spot proof
102 *Soria* Syria
106 *Lazaretto* pest-house; two were established in islands of the Gulf of Venice after the plagues of 1423 and 1576
110 *onions* supposed to protect against the plague by gathering the infection
111 *livre* French coin
114 *venture* invest in
115 *strain* stretch

I stick my onions, cut in halves: the other
Is full of loop-holes, out at which, I thrust
The noses of my bellows; and, those bellows
I keep, with water-works, in perpetual motion,
(Which is the easiest matter of a hundred). 120
Now, sir, your onion, which doth naturally
Attract th'infection, and your bellows, blowing
The air upon him, will show (instantly)
By his changed colour, if there be contagion,
Or else, remain as fair, as at the first. 125
Now 'tis known, 'tis nothing.

PEREGRINE You are right, sir.

SIR POLITIC
I would I had my note.

PEREGRINE Faith, so would I:
But, you ha' done well, for once, sir.

SIR POLITIC Were I false,
Or would be made so, I could show you reasons,
How I could sell this state, now, to the Turk; 130
Spite of their gallies, or their—

PEREGRINE Pray you, Sir Pol.

SIR POLITIC
I have 'em not, about me.

PEREGRINE That I feared.
They're there, sir?

SIR POLITIC No, this is my diary.
Wherein I note my actions of the day.

PEREGRINE
Pray you, let's see, sir. What is here? '*Notandum*, 135
A rat had gnawn my spur-leathers; notwithstanding,
I put on new, and did go forth: but, first,
I threw three beans over the threshold. *Item*,
I went, and bought two tooth-picks, whereof one
I burst, immediately, in a discourse 140
With a Dutch merchant, 'bout *ragion del stato*.
From him I went, and paid a *moccenigo*,

127 *note* perhaps the paper of line 84; possibly note of patent
128 *false* traitorous
131 *or their—* Sir Politic breaks off as he searches for his papers
136–138 *A rat . . . threshold* some details here are owed to Theophrastus's Character of a Superstitious Man
139 *tooth-picks* for the fashion of using toothpicks expressively see *King John* I. i, 190–193
141 *ragion del stato* reasons and affairs of state

For piecing my silk stockings; by the way,
I cheapened sprats: and at St. Mark's I urined.'
Faith, these are politic notes!

SIR POLITIC Sir, I do slip 145
No action of my life, thus, but I quote it.

PEREGRINE
Believe me it is wise!

SIR POLITIC Nay, sir, read forth.

Act IV, Scene ii

[*Enter* LADY WOULD-BE, NANO *and two* WOMEN]

LADY WOULD-BE
Where should this loose knight be, trow? sure, he's housed.

NANO
Why, then he's fast.

LADY WOULD-BE Ay, he plays both, with me:
I pray you, stay. This heat will do more harm
To my complexion, than his heart is worth.
(I do not care to hinder, but to take him) 5
How it comes off! [*Rubbing her face*]

1st WOMAN My master's yonder.

LADY WOULD-BE Where?

2nd WOMAN
With a young gentleman.

LADY WOULD-BE That same's the party!
In man's apparel. Pray you, sir, jog my knight:
I will be tender to his reputation,
However he demerit.

SIR POLITIC My lady?

PEREGRINE Where? 10

SIR POLITIC
'Tis she indeed, sir, you shall know her. She is,
Were she not mine, a lady of that merit,
For fashion, and behaviour; and, for beauty
I durst compare—

144 *cheapened sprats* by haggling; Coryat tells how Venetian gentlemen did their own shopping in the market, see p. 164
146 *quote* note
1 *loose* for the game of fast-and-loose, on which these lines pun, see I. ii, 8n.
1 *housed* i.e. with the 'cunning courtesan' of III. v, 20
5 *I do not care to* I am not anxious to
10 *demerit* merits blame

PEREGRINE It seems, you are not jealous,
That dare commend her.
SIR POLITIC Nay, and for discourse— 15
PEREGRINE
Being your wife, she cannot miss that.
SIR POLITIC [*The parties meet*] Madam,
Here is a gentleman, pray you, use him, fairly,
He seems a youth, but he is—
LADY WOULD-BE None?
SIR POLITIC Yes, one
Has put his face, as soon, into the world—
LADY WOULD-BE
You mean, as early? but today?
SIR POLITIC How's this! 20
LADY WOULD-BE
Why in this habit, sir, you apprehend me.
Well, Master Would-be, this doth not become you;
I had thought, the odour, sir, of your good name,
Had been more precious to you; that you would not
Have done this dire massacre, on your honour; 25
One of your gravity, and rank, besides!
But, knights, I see, care little for the oath
They make to ladies: chiefly, their own ladies.
SIR POLITIC
Now, by my spurs, the symbol of my knight-hood—
PEREGRINE [*Aside*]
Lord! how his brain is humbled, for an oath. 30
SIR POLITIC
I reach you not.
LADY WOULD-BE Right, sir, your polity
May bear it through, thus. [*To* PEREGRINE] Sir, a word with you.
I would be loath, to contest publicly,
With any gentlewoman; or to seem
Froward, or violent (as *The Courtier* says) 35

16 *miss* lack
19 *as soon* at so early an age; but the phrase is open to Lady Would-be's wilful misinterpretation
25 *massacre* accented on second syllable here
30 *humbled* brought low—down to his spurs; editors have here found a sneer at King James's readiness to create new knights (see *The Alchemist* II. ii, 86–87) 31 *reach* understand
31 *polity* policy, cunning bluff 32 *bear it through* carry it off
35 *Froward* refractory
35 *The Courtier* alluding to Castiglione, *The Courtier* Bk. 3

It comes too near rusticity, in a lady,
Which I would shun, by all means: and, however
I may deserve from Master Would-be, yet,
T'have one fair gentlewoman, thus, be made
Th'unkind instrument, to wrong another, 40
And one she knows not; ay, and to persever:
In my poor judgement, is not warranted
From being a solecism in our sex,
If not in manners.

PEREGRINE How is this!

SIR POLITIC Sweet madam,
Come nearer to your aim.

LADY WOULD-BE Marry, and will, sir. 45
Since you provoke me, with your impudence,
And laughter of your light land-siren, here,
Your Sporus, your hermaphrodite—

PEREGRINE What's here?
Poetic fury, and historic storms!

SIR POLITIC
The gentleman, believe it, is of worth, 50
And of our nation.

LADY WOULD-BE Ay, your Whitefriars nation!
Come, I blush for you, Master Would-be, I;
And am ashamed, you should ha' no more forehead,
Than, thus, to be the patron, or St. George
To a lewd harlot, a base fricatrice, 55
A female devil, in a male outside.

SIR POLITIC [*To* PEREGRINE] Nay,
And you be such a one, I must bid adieu
To your delights! The case appears too liquid.
[*Exit* SIR POLITIC]

41 *persever* accented on second syllable
43 *solecism* a grammatical, not a sexual, impropriety; the word is itself a solecism here
48 *Sporus* minion castrated and 'married' by Nero
49 *historic* perhaps 'epoch-making'
51 *Whitefriars nation* Whitefriars was a 'liberty' under the old priory charter, inside the City of London but outside its jurisdiction; it became almost a miniature state for outcasts
53 *forehead* 'capacity for blushing, modesty' (*OED*)
55 *fricatrice* whore (Latin *fricare*, to rub)
57 *you be* addressed either to Lady Would-be or to Peregrine
58 *case* possibly 'mask' or 'disguise'
58 *liquid* 'transparent, easily seen through' or 'amorphous, hard to grasp'; and Lady Would-be may be sobbing

LADY WOULD-BE
Ay, you may carry't clear, with your state-face!
But, for your carnival concupiscence, 60
Who here is fled for liberty of conscience,
From furious persecution of the marshal,
Her will I disple.

PEREGRINE This is fine, i'faith!
And do you use this, often? is this part
Of your wit's exercise, 'gainst you have occasion? 65
Madam—

LADY WOULD-BE Go to, sir.

PEREGRINE Do you hear me, lady?
Why, if your knight have set you to beg shirts,
Or to invite me home, you might have done it
A nearer way, by far.

LADY WOULD-BE This cannot work you,
Out of my snare.

PEREGRINE Why? am I in it, then? 70
Indeed, your husband told me, you were fair,
And so you are; only your nose inclines,
That side, that's next the sun, to the queen-apple.

LADY WOULD-BE
This cannot be endured, by any patience.

LX24

Act IV, Scene iii

[*Enter* MOSCA]

MOSCA
What's the matter, madam?

LADY WOULD-BE If the Senate

59 *state-face* politic countenance
60 *carnival* probably for 'carnal'
60 *concupiscence* for 'concupiscent (woman)'
61 *liberty of conscience* freedom from religious persecution; the prison marshal is conceived as the persecutor and concupiscence as the religion
63 *disple* ed. (FQ disc'ple) 'to subject to discipline; especially as a religious practice' (*OED*)
64 *use this* act like this
67 *beg shirts* Lady Would-be is evidently tugging at Peregrine's shirt
69 *nearer* more direct
73 *queen-apple* perhaps a quince, or early variety of apple; Lady Would-be's nose is red on one side (see III. iv, 16)

Right not my quest, in this; I will protest 'em,
To all the world, no aristocracy.

MOSCA
What is the injury, lady?

LADY WOULD-BE Why, the callet,
You told me of, here I have ta'en disguised. 5

MOSCA
Who? this? what means your ladyship? the creature
I mentioned to you, is apprehended, now,
Before the Senate, you shall see her—

LADY WOULD-BE Where?

MOSCA
I'll bring you to her. This young gentleman
I saw him land, this morning, at the port. 10

LADY WOULD-BE
Is't possible! how has my judgement wandered!
Sir, I must, blushing, say to you, I have erred:
And plead you pardon.

PEREGRINE What! more changes, yet?

LADY WOULD-BE
I hope, you ha'not the malice to remember
A gentlewoman's passion. If you stay, 15
In Venice, here, please you to use me, sir—

MOSCA
Will you go, madam?

LADY WOULD-BE Pray you, sir, use me. In faith,
The more you see me, the more I shall conceive,
You have forgot our quarrel.

PEREGRINE This is rare!
Sir Politic Would-be? no, Sir Politic Bawd! 20
To bring me, thus, acquainted with his wife!
Well, wise Sir Pol: since you have practised, thus,
Upon my freshmanship, I'll try your salt-head,
What proof it is against a counter-plot.

2 *quest* petition
2 *protest* proclaim
16 *use me* Lady Would-be intends to be socially useful but her rhetoric insinuates her readiness to be Peregrine's mistress
18 *conceive* understand; become pregnant
22 *practised* plotted; Peregrine thinks he has been gulled
23 *salt-head* seasoned, experienced; salacious, bawdy

Act IV, Scene iv

[*The Scrutineo*]

[*Enter*] VOLTORE, CORBACCIO, CORVINO, MOSCA

VOLTORE
Well, now you know the carriage of the business,
Your constancy is all, that is required
Unto the safety of it.

MOSCA
Is the lie
Safely conveyed amongst us? is that sure?
Knows every man his burden?

CORVINO
Yes.

MOSCA
Then, shrink not. 5

CORVINO [*Aside to* MOSCA]
But, knows the advocate the truth?

MOSCA
O, sir,
By no means. I devised a formal tale,
That salved your reputation. But, be valiant, sir.

CORVINO
I fear no one, but him; that, this his pleading
Should make him stand for a co-heir—

MOSCA
Co-halter. 10
Hang him: we will but use his tongue, his noise,
As we do Croaker's, here. [*Pointing to* CORBACCIO]

CORVINO
Ay, what shall he do?

1 *carriage* management
5 *burden* refrain of a song; hence 'part in the performance'
7 *formal* 'elaborately constructed, circumstantial' (*OED*)
8 *salved* healed, made good

12–20 de Vocht objects to the Folio directions (here inserted in round brackets) on the ground that they misinterpret the text. His remedial interventions, however, including the reassignment of 'I should . . . past' to Voltore, and the revision of line 20 with a redirection to Voltore ('But you shall eat it. Much worshipful sir,'), are as drastic as the Folio's and have no authority. I have retained the Folio interpretation from the conviction that Jonson at least tolerated it. The aside in line 16 is indicated in F by a dash only; although the diffidence seems uncharacteristic of Mosca it is not outside an actor's compass. Lines 17–19 are probably shouted at Corbaccio, for Corvino must overhear them if he is to make sense of line 20. Gifford and others since have read Mosca's 'Much!' of line 20 as an aside, but there is no reason why Voltore should not receive it as an ironic confidence—each gull supposes himself one up on the others.

MOSCA
When we ha' done, you mean?
CORVINO
Yes.
MOSCA
Why, we'll think:
Sell him for mummia, he's half dust already.
(*To* VOLTORE) Do not you smile, to see this buffalo, 15
[*Pointing to* CORVINO]
How he doth sport it with his head?—[*Aside*] I should
If all were well, and past. (*To* CORBACCIO) Sir, only you
Are he, that shall enjoy the crop of all,
And these not know for whom they toil.
CORBACCIO
Ay, peace.
MOSCA (*To* CORVINO)
But you shall eat it. (*then to* VOLTORE *again*) Much! 20
Worshipful sir,
Mercury sit upon your thund'ring tongue,
Or the French Hercules, and make your language
As conquering as his club, to beat along,
As with a tempest, flat, our adversaries:
But, much more, yours, sir.
VOLTORE
Here they come, ha' done. 25
MOSCA
I have another witness, if you need, sir,
I can produce.
VOLTORE
Who is it?
MOSCA
Sir, I have her.

Act IV, Scene v

[*Enter four* AVOCATORI, BONARIO, CELIA, NOTARIO, COMMENDATORI *and* OTHERS]

1st AVOCATORE
The like of this the Senate never heard of.

14 *mummia* a medicinal preparation from the substance of mummies; fake mummy was made from baked corpses
15 *buffalo* alluding to the cuckold's horns that the 'formal tale' sets upon Corvino
20 *eat it* i.e. the crop, the legacy; Corvino may overhear the words to Corbaccio
21 *Mercury* god of eloquence and of trade; also associated with trickery and theft
22 *French Hercules* Hercules was fabled to have fathered the Celts in Gaul while returning from the far west with the oxen of Geryon; as the Celtic Hercules he was the symbol of eloquence

2nd AVOCATORE
'Twill come most strange to them, when we report it.
4th AVOCATORE
The gentlewoman has been ever held
Of unreprovèd name.
3rd AVOCATORE So, the young man.
4th AVOCATORE
The more unnatural part that of his father. 5
2nd AVOCATORE
More of the husband.
1st AVOCATORE I not know to give
His act a name, it is so monstrous!
4th AVOCATORE
But the impostor, he is a thing created
T'exceed example!
1st AVOCATORE And all after times!
2nd AVOCATORE
I never heard a true voluptuary 10
Described, but him.
3rd AVOCATORE Appear yet those were cited?
NOTARIO
All, but the old magnifico, Volpone.
1st AVOCATORE
Why is not he here?
MOSCA Please your fatherhoods,
Here is his advocate. Himself's, so weak,
So feeble—
4th AVOCATORE What are you?
BONARIO His parasite, 15
His knave, his pandar: I beseech the court,
He may be forced to come, that your grave eyes
May bear strong witness of his strange impostures.
VOLTORE
Upon my faith, and credit, with your virtues,
He is not able to endure the air. 20
2nd AVOCATORE
Bring him, however.
3rd AVOCATORE We will see him.
4th AVOCATORE Fetch him.

4 *So, the young man* F (Q So has the youth)
9 *example* precedent
9 *after times* i.e. future possibilities
11 *cited* summoned, called as witnesses

VOLTORE

Your fatherhoods' fit pleasures be obeyed,
Be sure, the sight will rather move your pities,
Than indignation; may it please the court,
In the meantime, he may be heard in me: 25
I know this place most void of prejudice,
And therefore crave it, since we have no reason
To fear our truth should hurt our cause.

3rd AVOCATORE Speak free.

VOLTORE

Then know, most honoured fathers, I must now
Discover, to your strangely abusèd ears, 30
The most prodigious, and most frontless piece
Of solid impudence, and treachery,
That ever vicious nature yet brought forth
To shame the state of Venice. This lewd woman
(That wants no artificial looks, or tears, 35
To help the visor, she has now put on)
Hath long been known a close adulteress,
To that lascivious youth there; not suspected,
I say, but known; and taken, in the act,
With him; and by this man, the easy husband, 40
Pardoned: whose timeless bounty makes him, now,
Stand here, the most unhappy, innocent person,
That ever man's own goodness made accused.
For these, not knowing how to owe a gift
Of that dear grace, but with their shame; being placed 45
So above all powers of their gratitude,
Began to hate the benefit: and, in place
Of thanks, devise t'extirp the memory
Of such an act. Wherein, I pray your fatherhoods,

22 *fatherhoods* correct form of address, but for Voltore's exploitation of it see Volpone's reaction in V. ii, 33–37
31 *frontless* shameless
35 *wants* lacks
36 *visor* mask
37 *close* secret
41 *timeless* untimely
43 *goodness* F (Q vertue) see Introduction p. xiii
44 *owe* acknowledge (= own), or 'properly possess'
44–45 *gift . . . grace* 'so precious and unmerited a gift (of pardon)'
46 *So . . . gratitude* i.e. in a position of indebtedness beyond the reach of their powers of gratitude
48 *extirp* = extirpate, eradicate

To observe the malice, yea, the rage of creatures 50
Discovered in their evils; and what heart
Such take, even from their crimes. But that, anon,
Will more appear. This gentleman, the father,
Hearing of this foul fact, with many others,
Which daily struck at his too-tender ears, 55
And, grieved in nothing more, than that he could not
Preserve himself a parent (his son's ills
Growing to that strange flood) at last decreed
To disinherit him.

1st AVOCATORE These be strange turns!

2nd AVOCATORE
The young man's fame was ever fair, and honest. 60

VOLTORE
So much more full of danger is his vice,
That can beguile so, under shade of virtue.
But as I said, my honoured sires, his father
Having this settled purpose, (by what means
To him betrayed, we know not) and this day 65
Appointed for the deed; that parricide,
(I cannot style him better) by confederacy
Preparing this his paramour to be there,
Entered Volpone's house (who was the man
Your fatherhoods must understand, designed 70
For the inheritance) there sought his father:
But, with what purpose sought he him, my lords?
(I tremble to pronounce it, that a son
Unto a father, and to such a father
Should have so foul, felonious intent) 75
It was, to murder him. When, being prevented
By his more happy absence, what then did he?
Not check his wicked thoughts; no, now new deeds:
(Mischief doth ever end, where it begins)
An act of horror, fathers! he dragged forth 80
The agèd gentleman, that had there lain, bed-rid,
Three years, and more, out of his innocent couch,
Naked, upon the floor, there left him; wounded

51 *heart* hardness of heart; impudent courage
57 *ills* evils
59 *turns* turns of event
67 *confederacy* conspiracy
70 *designed* designated
79 *ever* the reading 'never' has been proposed and followed by some editors, but 'ever' means 'what begins badly ends badly'

His servant in the face; and, with this strumpet,
The stale to his forged practice, who was glad 85
To be so active, (I shall here desire
Your fatherhoods to note but my collections,
As most remarkable) thought, at once, to stop
His father's ends; discredit his free choice,
In the old gentleman; redeem themselves, 90
By laying infamy upon this man,
To whom, with blushing, they should owe their lives.

1st AVOCATORE
What proofs have you of this?

BONARIO
Most honoured fathers,
I humbly crave, there be no credit given
To this man's mercenary tongue.

2nd AVOCATORE
Forbear. 95

BONARIO
His soul moves in his fee.

3rd AVOCATORE
O, sir.

BONARIO
This fellow,
For six sols more, would plead against his maker.

1st AVOCATORE
You do forget yourself.

VOLTORE
Nay, nay, grave fathers,
Let him have scope: can any man imagine
That he will spare his accuser, that would not 100
Have spared his parent?

1st AVOCATORE
Well, produce your proofs.

CELIA
I would I could forget, I were a creature.

VOLTORE
Signior Corbaccio.

4th AVOCATORE
What is he?

VOLTORE
The father.

2nd AVOCATORE
Has he had an oath?

85 *stale* lure; 'a prostitute of the lowest class employed as a decoy by thieves' (*OED*)
85 *forged practice* contrived plot
87 *collections* conclusions
89 *ends* purposes, aims
90 *gentleman* i.e. Volpone
92 *owe* acknowledge as due
97 *sols* French coins worth one twentieth of a livre
102 *creature* compare III. vii, 246; 'one of God's creatures'; 'a creature of circumstance'

NOTARIO Yes.

CORBACCIO What must I do now?

NOTARIO
Your testimony's craved.

CORBACCIO Speak to the knave? 105
I'll ha' my mouth, first, stopped with earth; my heart
Abhors his knowledge: I disclaim in him.

1st AVOCATORE
But, for what cause?

CORBACCIO The mere portent of nature.
He is an utter stranger, to my loins.

BONARIO
Have they made you to this!

CORBACCIO I will not hear thee, 110
Monster of men, swine, goat, wolf, parricide,
Speak not, thou viper.

BONARIO Sir, I will sit down,
And rather wish my innocence should suffer,
Than I resist the authority of a father.

VOLTORE
Signior Corvino.

2nd AVOCATORE This is strange!

1st AVOCATORE Who's this? 115

NOTARIO
The husband.

4th AVOCATORE Is he sworn?

NOTARIO He is.

3rd AVOCATORE Speak then.

CORVINO
This woman, please your fatherhoods, is a whore,
Of most hot exercise, more than a partridge,
Upon record—

1st AVOCATORE No more.

CORVINO Neighs, like a jennet.

NOTARIO
Preserve the honour of the court.

107 *his knowledge* knowledge of him
107 *disclaim* deny kinship
108 *portent* ominous freak; suggesting unnatural birth and leading to the denial of paternity
110 *made* forced, or possibly 'shaped'
118 *partridge* described by Pliny as the most concupiscent of creatures (*Nat. Hist.* X. 102)
119 *jennet* small Spanish horse

CORVINO I shall, 120
And modesty of your most reverend ears.
And yet, I hope that I may say, these eyes
Have seen her glued unto that piece of cedar;
That fine well-timbered gallant: and that, here,
The letters may be read, thorough the horn, 125
That make the story perfect.

MOSCA Excellent! sir.

CORVINO
There is no shame in this, now, is there?

MOSCA None.

CORVINO
Or if I said, I hoped that she were onward
To her damnation, if there be a hell
Greater than whore, and woman; a good Catholic 130
May make the doubt.

3rd AVOCATORE His grief hath made him frantic.

1st AVOCATORE
Remove him, hence.

2nd AVOCATORE Look to the woman. *She swoons*

CORVINO Rare!
Prettily feigned! again!

4th AVOCATORE Stand from about her.

1st AVOCATORE
Give her the air.

3rd AVOCATORE [*To* MOSCA] What can you say?

MOSCA My wound,
May't please your wisdoms, speaks for me, received 135
In aid of my good patron, when he missed
His sought-for father, when that well-taught dame
Had her cue given her, to cry out a rape.

BONARIO
O, most laid impudence! Fathers—

124 *well-timbered* well-built
124 *here* Corvino holds his forked fingers to his forehead to give himself cuckold's horns
125 *letters . . . horn* punning on 'horn-book', a primer (so-called because protected by translucent horn) 126 *perfect* complete
127 *shame* F (Q harm) 'shame' is the more ironic word
128 *onward* well on the way
130 *Catholic* F (Q Christian) perhaps when Jonson was a Catholic he preferred to assign this heretical sentiment less specifically; but perhaps the F reading is to fit the Venetian scene
139 *laid* plotted

3rd AVOCATORE Sir, be silent,
You had your hearing free, so must they theirs. 140
2nd AVOCATORE
I do begin to doubt th'imposture here.
4th AVOCATORE
This woman, has too many moods.
VOLTORE Grave fathers,
She is a creature, of a most professed,
And prostituted lewdness.
CORVINO Most impetuous!
Unsatisfied, grave fathers!
VOLTORE May her feignings 145
Not take your wisdoms: but this day, she baited
A stranger, a grave knight, with her loose eyes,
And more lascivious kisses. This man saw 'em
Together, on the water, in a gondola.
MOSCA
Here is the lady herself, that saw 'em too, 150
Without; who, then, had in the open streets
Pursued them, but for saving her knight's honour.
1st AVOCATORE
Produce that lady.
2nd AVOCATORE Let her come. [*Exit* MOSCA]
4th AVOCATORE These things
They strike, with wonder!
3rd AVOCATORE I am turned a stone!

Act IV, Scene vi

[*Enter* MOSCA *with* LADY WOULD-BE]

MOSCA
Be resolute, madam.
LADY WOULD-BE Ay, this same is she.
Out, thou chameleon harlot: now, thine eyes
Vie tears with the hyaena: dar'st thou look

140 *free* i.e. from interruption
146 *baited* enticed
151 *Without* outside
2 *chameleon* its colour changes made it a symbol of fraud and treachery; Lady Would-be alludes to the inconstant appearance of her quarry
3 *hyaena* another symbol of treachery because it attracted its victims by its quasi-human cry (but not by its tears)

Upon my wrongèd face? I cry your pardons.
I fear, I have, forgettingly, transgressed 5
Against the dignity of the court—

2nd AVOCATORE No, madam.

LADY WOULD-BE
And been exorbitant—

4th AVOCATORE You have not, lady.
These proofs are strong.

LADY WOULD-BE Surely, I had no purpose,
To scandalize your honours, or my sex's.

3rd AVOCATORE
We do believe it.

LADY WOULD-BE Surely, you may believe it. 10

2nd AVOCATORE
Madam, we do.

LADY WOULD-BE Indeed, you may; my breeding
Is not so coarse—

4th AVOCATORE We know it.

LADY WOULD-BE To offend
With pertinacy—

3rd AVOCATORE Lady.

LADY WOULD-BE Such a presence:
No, surely.

1st AVOCATORE We well think it.

LADY WOULD-BE You may think it.

1st AVOCATORE
Let her o'ercome. [*To* BONARIO] What witnesses have you, 15
To make good your report?

BONARIO Our consciences—

CELIA
And heaven, that never fails the innocent.

4th AVOCATORE
These are no testimonies.

BONARIO Not in your courts,
Where multitude, and clamour, overcomes.

1st AVOCATORE
Nay, then you do wax insolent.

7 *exorbitant* beyond bounds, outrageous
13 *pertinacy* FQ (eds. pertinency); old form of 'pertinacity'; but Lady Would-be apparently intends 'impertinacy', an erroneous form of 'impertinence'
15 *o'ercome* prevail, have the last word
19 *multitude* numbers (not necessarily a crowd)

VOLTORE
Here, here, 20

VOLPONE *is brought in, as impotent*

The testimony comes, that will convince,
And put to utter dumbness their bold tongues.
See here, grave fathers, here's the ravisher,
The rider on men's wives, the great impostor,
The grand voluptuary! do you not think, 25
These limbs should affect venery? or these eyes
Covet a concubine? pray you, mark these hands.
Are they not fit to stroke a lady's breasts?
Perhaps, he doth dissemble?

BONARIO
So he does.

VOLTORE
Would you ha'him tortured?

BONARIO
I would have him proved. 30

VOLTORE
Best try him, then, with goads, or burning irons;
Put him to the strappado: I have heard,
The rack hath cured the gout, faith, give it him,
And help him of a malady, be courteous.
I'll undertake, before these honoured fathers, 35
He shall have, yet, as many left diseases,
As she has known adulterers, or thou strumpets.
O, my most equal hearers, if these deeds,
Acts, of this bold, and most exorbitant strain,
May pass with sufferance, what one citizen, 40
But owes the forfeit of his life, yea fame,
To him that dares traduce him? which of you
Are safe, my honoured fathers? I would ask,

20 s.d. *impotent* totally disabled; Lady Would-be may kiss Volpone at this point (see V. ii, 97), or when he is borne out
26 *affect venery* enjoy sexual pleasure; or 'affect' may = 'effect'
30 *proved* put to the proof, tested
32 *strappado* a form of torture; the victim is hoisted by a rope binding his wrists behind his back, then dropped with a jerk; Coryat reports the practice in Venice (see p. 164
33 *rack . . . gout* a common sentiment (e.g. Marston, *Malcontent* III. i, 70)
34 *help* relieve
38 *equal* just
39 *exorbitant strain* outrageous nature
40–42 *what . . . traduce him* 'what single citizen would there be whose life, and indeed reputation, would not be forfeitable to any who had the impudence to slander him?'

With leave of your grave fatherhoods, if their plot
Have any face, or colour like to truth? 45
Or if, unto the dullest nostril, here,
It smell not rank, and most abhorred slander?
I crave your care of this good gentleman,
Whose life is much endangered, by their fable;
And, as for them, I will conclude with this, 50
That vicious persons when they are hot, and fleshed
In impious acts, their constancy abounds:
Damned deeds are done with greatest confidence.

1st AVOCATORE
Take 'em to custody, and sever them.
[CELIA *and* BONARIO *taken out*]

2nd AVOCATORE
'Tis pity, two such prodigies should live. 55

1st AVOCATORE
Let the old gentleman be returned, with care:
I'm sorry, our credulity wronged him. [VOLPONE *borne off*]

4th AVOCATORE
These are two creatures!

3rd AVOCATORE I have an earthquake in me!

2nd AVOCATORE
Their shame, even in their cradles, fled their faces.

4th AVOCATORE
You've done a worthy service to the state, sir, 60
In their discovery.

1st AVOCATORE You shall hear, ere night,
What punishment the court decrees upon 'em.

VOLTORE
We thank your fatherhoods.
[*Exeunt* AVOCATORI, NOTARIO, OFFICERS]
How like you it?

MOSCA Rare.
I'd ha'your tongue, sir, tipped with gold, for this;
I'd ha'you be the heir to the whole city; 65
The earth I'd have want men, ere you want living:
They're bound to erect your statue, in St. Mark's.

49 *fable* falsehood, or plot
51 *fleshed* inured
52 *constancy* resolution; recalling Juvenal, *Satires* XIII. 237–240
54 *sever them* keep them apart
55 *prodigies* monsters, unnatural creatures (compare 'portent', IV. v, 108)
66 *want living* lack a livelihood

Signior Corvino, I would have you go,
And show yourself, that you have conquered.

CORVINO Yes.

MOSCA
It was much better, that you should profess 70
Yourself a cuckold, thus; than that the other
Should have been proved.

CORVINO Nay, I considered that:
Now, it is her fault—

MOSCA Then, it had been yours.

CORVINO
True, I do doubt this advocate, still.

MOSCA I'faith,
You need not, I dare ease you of that care. 75

CORVINO
I trust thee, Mosca.

MOSCA As your own soul, sir.

CORBACCIO Mosca!

MOSCA
Now for your business, sir.

CORBACCIO How? ha'you business?

MOSCA
Yes, yours, sir.

CORBACCIO O, none else?

MOSCA None else, not I.

CORBACCIO
Be careful then.

MOSCA Rest you, with both your eyes, sir.

CORBACCIO
Dispatch it—

MOSCA Instantly.

CORBACCIO And look, that all, 80
Whatever, be put in, jewels, plate, monies,
Household stuff, bedding, curtains.

MOSCA Curtain-rings, sir,
Only, the advocate's fee must be deducted.

CORBACCIO
I'll pay him now: you'll be too prodigal.

MOSCA
Sir, I must tender it.

71 *the other* i.e. the procuration of his wife for Volpone
79 *Rest . . . eyes* 'relax completely'
81 *put in* i.e. in the inventory of the inheritance
85 *tender it* give it him

CORBACCIO Two chequeens is well? 85
MOSCA
No, six, sir.
CORBACCIO 'Tis too much.
MOSCA He talked a great while,
You must consider that, sir.
CORBACCIO Well, there's three—
MOSCA I'll give it him.
CORBACCIO Do so, and there's for thee.
[*Exit* CORBACCIO]
MOSCA
Bountiful bones! What horrid strange offence
Did he commit 'gainst nature, in his youth, 90
Worthy his age? you see, sir, how I work
Unto your ends; take you no notice.
VOLTORE No,
I'll leave you.
MOSCA All is yours; [*Exit* VOLTORE] the devil, and all:
Good advocate.—Madame, I'll bring you home.
LADY WOULD-BE
No, I'll go see your patron.
MOSCA That you shall not: 95
I'll tell you, why. My purpose is, to urge
My patron to reform his will; and, for
The zeal you've shown today, whereas before
You were but third, or fourth, you shall be now
Put in the first: which would appear as begged, 100
If you were present. Therefore—
LADY WOULD-BE You shall sway me.
[*Exeunt* MOSCA, LADY WOULD-BE]

89 *Bountiful bones!* apt to the meanness and leanness of Corbaccio
91 *Worthy . . . age* 'deserving an old age like this'
92 *take . . . notice* 'ignore me'; perhaps Lady Would-be is watching
97 *reform* recast
101 *sway* rule

Act V, Scene i

[VOLPONE's *House*]

[*Enter*] VOLPONE

VOLPONE
Well, I am here; and all this brunt is past:
I ne'er was in dislike with my disguise,
Till this fled moment; here, 'twas good, in private,
But, in your public—*Cavè*, whilst I breathe. [*Gets up*]
'Fore God, my left leg 'gan to have the cramp; 5
And I apprehended, straight, some power had struck me
With a dead palsy: well, I must be merry,
And shake it off. A many of these fears
Would put me into some villainous disease,
Should they come thick upon me: I'll prevent 'em. 10
Give me a bowl of lusty wine, to fright
This humour from my heart. (*He drinks*) Hum, hum, hum!
'Tis almost gone, already: I shall conquer.
Any device, now, of rare, ingenious knavery,
That would possess me with a violent laughter, 15
Would make me up, again! (*Drinks again*) So, so, so, so.
This heat is life; 'tis blood, by this time: Mosca!

Act V, Scene ii

[*Enter* MOSCA]

MOSCA
How now, sir? does the day look clear again?
Are we recovered? and wrought out of error,

s.d. *Enter Volpone* Volpone may be carried in, discovered on his litter, or be back in his bed
1 *brunt* shock, crisis
3 *fled* past
4 *Cavè* (Latin) beware; Volpone may ask the audience to keep a look-out while he relaxes, or he may address the warning to himself
6 *apprehended* F (Q apprêhended) felt
6 *straight* immediately
8 *many* used as a noun (compare 'a great many')
17 *This heat is life* Volpone identifies the response of his blood to wine with the processes by which the body's vital heat is generated
2–3 *wrought . . . way* Mosca talks with mock piety (see, e.g., *James* V. 20)

Into our way? to see our path, before us?
Is our trade free, once more?

VOLPONE
Exquisite Mosca!

MOSCA
Was it not carried learnedly?

VOLPONE
And stoutly. 5
Good wits are greatest in extremities.

MOSCA
It were a folly, beyond thought, to trust
Any grand act unto a cowardly spirit:
You are not taken with it, enough, methinks?

VOLPONE
O, more, than if I had enjoyed the wench: 10
The pleasure of all woman-kind's not like it.

MOSCA
Why, now you speak, sir. We must, here, be fixed;
Here, we must rest; this is our masterpiece:
We cannot think, to go beyond this.

VOLPONE
True,
Thou'st played thy prize, my precious Mosca.

MOSCA
Nay, sir, 15
To gull the court—

VOLPONE
And, quite divert the torrent
Upon the innocent.

MOSCA
Yes, and to make
So rare a music out of discords—

VOLPONE
Right,
That, yet, to me's the strangest! how thou'st borne it!
That these, being so divided 'mongst themselves, 20
Should not scent somewhat, or in me, or thee,
Or doubt their own side.

MOSCA
True, they will not see't.
Too much light blinds 'em, I think. Each of 'em
Is so possessed, and stuffed with his own hopes,
That anything, unto the contrary, 25
Never so true, or never so apparent,
Never so palpable, they will resist it—

9 *You . . . enough* Mosca may sense that Volpone is already thinking of the next device, towards which the dialogue now subtly moves

19 *strangest* most wonderful and ingenious; the word 'strange' is important in this act 21 *or . . . or* either . . . or

24 *possessed* the sense hovers between 'possessing' and 'possessed by'; another key word

VOLPONE

Like a temptation of the devil.

MOSCA Right, sir.

Merchants may talk of trade, and your great signiors
Of land, that yields well; but if Italy 30
Have any glebe, more fruitful, than these fellows,
I am deceived. Did not your advocate rare?

VOLPONE

O—'My most honoured fathers, my grave fathers,
Under correction of your fatherhoods,
What face of truth, is here? If these strange deeds 35
May pass, most honoured fathers'—I had much ado
To forbear laughing.

MOSCA 'T seemed to me, you sweat, sir.

VOLPONE

In troth, I did a little.

MOSCA But confess, sir,
Were you not daunted?

VOLPONE In good faith, I was
A little in a mist; but not dejected: 40
Never, but still myself.

MOSCA I think it, sir.
Now, so truth help me, I must needs say this, sir,
And, out of conscience, for your advocate:
He's taken pains, in faith, sir, and deserved,
(In my poor judgement, I speak it, under favour, 45
Not to contrary you, sir) very richly—
Well—to be cozened.

VOLPONE 'Troth, and I think so too,
By that I heard him, in the latter end.

MOSCA

O, but before, sir; had you heard him, first,
Draw it to certain heads, then aggravate, 50

31 *glebe* earth, soil 32 *rare* rarely

37 *sweat* sweated; Mosca insists that Volpone was afraid

39–40 *daunted* 'dazed' or 'abashed'; Volpone's reply meets both senses, he was a little confused (*in a mist*) but not downcast (*dejected*) 41 *think* believe

45 *under favour* 'with your permission'; Mosca now parodies Voltore

47 *cozened* cheated; Mosca's anticlimax is itself a 'vehement figure' (line 51)

50 *heads* chief points of a discourse (*OED*), e.g. Voltore's 'collections' at IV. v, 86–92

50 *aggravate* put weight upon, solemnly emphasise with *gravitas*

Then use his vehement figures—I looked still,
When he would shift a shirt; and, doing this
Out of pure love, no hope of gain—

VOLPONE 'Tis right.
I cannot answer him, Mosca, as I would,
Not yet; but, for thy sake, at thy entreaty, 55
I will begin, even now, to vex 'em all:
This very instant.

MOSCA Good, sir.

VOLPONE Call the dwarf,
And eunuch, forth.

MOSCA Castrone, Nano!

[*Enter* CASTRONE *and* NANO]

NANO Here.

VOLPONE
Shall we have a jig, now?

MOSCA What you please, sir.

VOLPONE Go,
Straight, give out, about the streets, you two, 60
That I am dead; do it with constancy,
Sadly, do you hear? impute it to the grief
Of this late slander. [*Exeunt* CASTRONE *and* NANO]

MOSCA What do you mean, sir?

VOLPONE O,
I shall have, instantly, my vulture, crow,
Raven, come flying hither, on the news, 65
To peck for carrion, my she-wolf, and all,
Greedy, and full of expectation—

MOSCA
And then to have it ravished from their mouths?

VOLPONE
'Tis true, I will ha' thee put on a gown,

51 *vehement figures* may refer to figures of both speech and gesture
52 *shift a shirt* change a shirt; a figure for Voltore's gesticulations
53 *pure love* e.g. IV. vi, 48–49, where Voltore expresses solicitude for Volpone's life
54 *answer* repay
59 *a jig* a jest, 'some sport'; a burlesque 'jig' sometimes followed serious drama in the Elizabethan theatre, which may be the point here
61 *with constancy* firmly, or perhaps 'with straight faces'
62 *Sadly* gravely
63 *mean* intend

And take upon thee, as thou wert mine heir; 70
Show 'em a will: open that chest, and reach
Forth one of those, that has the blanks. I'll straight
Put in thy name.

MOSCA It will be rare, sir.

VOLPONE Ay,
When they e'en gape, and find themselves deluded—

MOSCA
Yes.

VOLPONE And thou use them scurvily. Dispatch, 75
Get on thy gown.

MOSCA But, what, sir, if they ask
After the body?

VOLPONE Say, it was corrupted.

MOSCA
I'll say it stunk, sir; and was fain t'have it
Coffined up instantly, and sent away.

VOLPONE
Anything, what thou wilt. Hold, here's my will. 80
Get thee a cap, a count-book, pen and ink,
Papers afore thee; sit, as thou wert taking
An inventory of parcels: I'll get up,
Behind the curtain, on a stool, and hearken;
Sometime, peep over; see, how they do look; 85
With what degrees, their blood doth leave their faces!
O, 'twill afford me a rare meal of laughter.

MOSCA
Your advocate will turn stark dull, upon it.

VOLPONE
It will take off his oratory's edge.

MOSCA
But your *clarissimo*, old round-back, he 90
Will crump you, like a hog-louse, with the touch.

VOLPONE
And what Corvino?

MOSCA O, sir, look for him,

70 *take upon thee* assume the part
72 *has* i.e. have
72 *blanks* spaces for the legatee's names
74 *e'en* just, doing nothing else but
78 *fain* i.e. 'I was fain (obliged)'
81 *count-book* account book
83 *parcels* lots, items
88 *dull* insensible; but Volpone replies to the sense 'blunt'
90 *clarissimo* a Venetian grandee
91 *crump . . . louse* 'curl up like a wood-louse'; 'you' is ethic dative

Tomorrow morning, with a rope, and a dagger,
To visit all the streets; he must run mad.
My lady too, that came into the court, 95
To bear false witness, for your worship—

VOLPONE
Yes,
And kissed me 'fore the fathers; when my face
Flowed all with oils—

MOSCA
And sweat, sir. Why, your gold
Is such another medicine, it dries up
All those offensive savours! It transforms 100
The most deformed, and restores 'em lovely,
As 'twere the strange poetical girdle. Jove
Could not invent, t' himself, a shroud more subtle,
To pass Acrisius' guards. It is the thing
Makes all the world her grace, her youth, her beauty. 105

VOLPONE
I think, she loves me.

MOSCA
Who? the lady, sir?
She's jealous of you.

VOLPONE
Do'st thou say so? [*Knocking without*]

MOSCA
Hark,
There's some already.

VOLPONE
Look.

MOSCA
It is the vulture:
He has the quickest scent.

VOLPONE
I'll to my place, [*Conceals himself*]
Thou, to thy posture.

MOSCA
I am set.

VOLPONE
But, Mosca, desk ? — 110
Play the artificer now, torture 'em, rarely.

93 *rope . . . dagger* stock properties of suicidal or homicidal madness induced by despair; compare Hieronimo's madness (once played by Jonson) in *The Spanish Tragedy* IV.iv
97 *kissed me* see IV. vi, 20 s.d. note
98–105 *your gold . . . her beauty* imitates Lucian, *Gallus* 722
102 *poetical girdle* the Folio adds the explanation '*Cestus*' after 'Jove'; it was possibly meant as a correction to replace 'girdle'; Cestus, the girdle of Venus described by Homer (*Iliad* XIV. 214–216), could transfigure ugliness and awaken passion even in old age
104 *Acrisius* the father of Danae; he shut her in a tower of brass but Jove reached her in a shower of gold
106 *the lady* presumably Lady Would-be, but some have supposed Celia
110 *posture* pose, act
111 *Play the artificer* 'do a craftsman's job', with pun on the sense 'trickster'

Act V, Scene iii

[*Enter* VOLTORE]

VOLTORE
How now, my Mosca?
MOSCA Turkey carpets, nine—
VOLTORE
Taking an inventory? that is well.
MOSCA
Two suits of bedding, tissue—
VOLTORE Where's the will?
Let me read that, the while.

[*Enter* CORBACCIO *carried in a chair*]

CORBACCIO So, set me down:
And get you home. [*Exeunt* PORTERS]
VOLTORE Is he come, now, to trouble us? 5
MOSCA Of cloth of gold, two more—
CORBACCIO Is it done, Mosca?
MOSCA
Of several velvets, eight—
VOLTORE I like his care.
CORBACCIO
Dost thou not hear?

[*Enter* CORVINO]

CORVINO Ha! is the hour come, Mosca?

→ window VOLPONE *peeps from behind a traverse*

VOLPONE [*Aside*]
Ay, now they muster.
CORVINO What does the advocate here?
Or this Corbaccio?
CORBACCIO What do these here?

[*Enter* LADY WOULD-BE]

1 *Turkey carpets* then used as table and wall drapery
3 *tissue* cloth woven with gold or silver
7 *velvets* ed. (FQ vellets); velvet hangings (several = separate)
8 s.d. *traverse* see Introduction p. xxx

LADY WOULD-BE Mosca! 10
Is his thread spun?
MOSCA Eight chests of linen—
VOLPONE [*Aside*] O,
My fine dame Would-be, too!
CORVINO Mosca, the will,
That I may show it these, and rid 'em hence.
MOSCA
Six chests of diaper, four of damask—There
[*Gives them the will*]
CORBACCIO
Is that the will?
MOSCA Down-beds, and bolsters—
VOLPONE [*Aside*] Rare! 15
Be busy still. Now, they begin to flutter:
They never think of me. Look, see, see, see!
How their swift eyes run over the long deed,
Unto the name, and to the legacies,
What is bequeathed them, there—
MOSCA Ten suits of hangings— 20
VOLPONE [*Aside*]
Ay, i'their garters, Mosca. Now, their hopes
Are at the gasp.
VOLTORE Mosca the heir!
CORBACCIO What's that?
VOLPONE [*Aside*]
My advocate is dumb, look to my merchant,
He has heard of some strange storm, a ship is lost,
He faints: my lady will swoon. Old glazen-eyes, 25
He hath not reached his despair, yet.
CORBACCIO All these
Are out of hope, I am sure the man.
CORVINO But, Mosca—

11 *thread* of the Three Fates, Clothos spun the thread of life, Lachesis measured it, and Atropos cut it; but the phrase was a popular pomposity (see *2 Henry VI* IV. ii, 31, where one of Cade's men uses it)
14 *diaper* fabric with diamond-like pattern
20 *suits of hangings* sets for four-poster bed (which may also be meant by 'suits of bedding' in line 3)
21 *garters* Volpone puns on the popular jibe 'Hang yourself in your own garters' (see *1 Henry IV* II. ii, 46)
22 *gasp* last gasp
25 *glazen-eyes* Corbaccio wears spectacles (see line 63, below)

MOSCA
Two cabinets—
CORVINO Is this in earnest?
MOSCA One
Of ebony—
CORVINO Or, do you but delude me?
MOSCA
The other, mother of pearl—I am very busy. 30
Good faith, it is a fortune thrown upon me—
Item, one salt of agate—not my seeking.
LADY WOULD-BE
Do you hear, sir?
MOSCA A perfumed box—'pray you forbear,
You see I am troubled—made of an onyx—
LADY WOULD-BE How!
MOSCA
Tomorrow, or next day, I shall be at leisure, 35
To talk with you all.
CORVINO Is this my large hope's issue?
LADY WOULD-BE
Sir, I must have a fairer answer.
MOSCA Madam!
Marry, and shall: pray you, fairly quit my house.
Nay, raise no tempest with your looks; but, hark you:
Remember, what your ladyship offered me, 40
To put you in, an heir; go to, think on't.
And what you said, e'en your best madams did
For maintenance, and why not you? enough.
Go home, and use the poor Sir Pol, your knight, well;
For fear I tell some riddles: go, be melancholic. 45
[*Exit* LADY WOULD-BE]
VOLPONE [*Aside*]
O, my fine devil!
CORVINO Mosca, pray you a word.
MOSCA
Lord! will not you take your dispatch hence, yet?
Methinks, of all, you should have been th'example.

32 *salt* salt-cellar
34 *troubled* busy, being put to some trouble; or perhaps 'vexed'
38 *fairly* probably 'well and truly', completely
40–43 *Remember . . . you* these lines supply the plot initiated at IV. vi, 96–101
45 *riddles* mysteries, secrets
48 *example* i.e. in leading the way when 'dispatched'

Why should you stay, here? with what thought? what promise?
Hear you, do not you know, I know you an ass? 50
And that you would, most fain, have been a wittol,
If fortune would have let you? that you are
A declared cuckold, on good terms? this pearl,
You'll say, was yours? right: this diamant?
I'll not deny't, but thank you. Much here, else? 55
It may be so. Why, think that these good works
May help to hide your bad: I'll not betray you,
Although you be but extraordinary,
And have it only in title, if sufficeth.
Go home, be melancholic too, or mad. [*Exit* CORVINO] 60

VOLPONE [*Aside*]
Rare, Mosca! how this villainy becomes him!

VOLTORE
Certain, he doth delude all these, for me.

CORBACCIO
Mosca, the heir?

VOLPONE [*Aside*] O, his four eyes have found it!

CORBACCIO
I'm cozened, cheated, by a parasite slave;
Harlot thou'st gulled me.

MOSCA Yes, sir. Stop your mouth, 65
Or I shall draw the only tooth, is left.
Are not you he, that filthy covetous wretch,
With the three legs, that here, in hope of prey,
Have, any time this three year, snuffed about,
With your most grov'ling nose; and would have hired 70
Me to the poisoning of my patron? sir?
Are not you he, that have, today, in court,
Professed the disinheriting of your son?
Perjured yourself? Go home, and die, and stink;
If you but croak a syllable, all comes out: 75
Away and call your porters, go, go, stink. [*Exit* CORBACCIO]

VOLPONE [*Aside*]
Excellent varlet!

51 *wittol* conniving cuckold
53 *on good terms* i.e. outspokenly so, fair and square
58 *extraordinary* in title only (as Mosca explains); used of offices held extra to the establishment
65 *Harlot* base-born fellow
68 *three legs* i.e. with his stick; in the riddle of the Sphinx, the child goes upon four legs, the man on two, and the old man on three

VOLTORE Now, my faithful Mosca,
I find thy constancy—
MOSCA Sir?
VOLTORE Sincere.
MOSCA A table
Of porphyry—I mar'l, you'll be thus troublesome.
VOLTORE
Nay, leave off now, they are gone.
MOSCA Why, who are you? 80
What, who did send for you? O, cry your mercy,
Reverend sir! good faith, I am grieved for you,
That any chance of mine should thus defeat
Your, I must needs say, most deserving travails:
But, I protest, sir, it was cast upon me, 85
And I could, almost, wish to be without it,
But that the will o'the dead, must be observed.
Marry, my joy is, that you need it not,
You have a gift, sir, thank your education,
Will never let you want, while there are men, 90
And malice, to breed causes. Would I had
But half the like, for all my fortune, sir.
If I have any suits (as I do hope,
Things being so easy, and direct, I shall not)
I will make bold with your obstreperous aid, 95
Conceive me, for your fee, sir. In meantime,
You, that have so much law, I know ha' the conscience,
Not to be covetous of what is mine.
Good sir, I thank you for my plate: 'twill help
To set up a young man. Good faith, you look 100
As you were costive; best go home, and purge, sir.
[*Exit* VOLTORE]
VOLPONE [*Coming out*]
Bid him, eat lettuce well: my witty mischief,
Let me embrace thee. O, that I could now
Transform thee to a Venus—Mosca, go,

79 *mar'l* marvel
83 *chance* good fortune
90 *want* be in need
91 *causes* law-suits
95 *obstreperous* vociferous
96 *Conceive . . . fee* 'I shall expect to pay the usual fee, you understand'
99 *plate* i.e. that presented by Voltore (I. iii, 10)
102 *lettuce* a recognised treatment for constipation, and for frenzy

Straight, take my habit of *clarissimo*; 105
And walk the streets; be seen, torment 'em more:
We must pursue, as well as plot. Who would
Have lost this feast?

MOSCA I doubt it will lose them.

VOLPONE
O, my recovery shall recover all.
That I could now but think on some disguise, 110
To meet 'em in: and ask 'em questions.
How I would vex 'em still, at every turn!

MOSCA
Sir, I can fit you.

VOLPONE Canst thou?

MOSCA Yes, I know
One o' the *commendatori*, sir, so like you,
Him will I straight make drunk, can bring you his habit. 115

VOLPONE
A rare disguise, and answering thy brain!
O, I will be a sharp disease unto 'em.

MOSCA
Sir, you must look for curses—

VOLPONE Till they burst;
The Fox fares ever best, when he is cursed.

Act V, Scene iv

[SIR POLITIC WOULD-BE'*s House*]

[*Enter* PEREGRINE *disguised, and three* MERCHANTS]

PEREGRINE
Am I enough disguised?

1st MERCHANT I warrant you.

PEREGRINE
All my ambition is to fright him, only.

105 *habit of clarissimo* for a description see p. 164
108 *doubt . . . them* possibly 'I doubt if it will get rid of them', but Volpone's reply interprets 'I fear it will lose them to us as a source of income'
114 *commendatori* ed. (F Commandatori Q Commandadori) a term for the court officers, sergeants at law
119 *Fox . . . cursed* a proverb; the fox is only cursed by the hunter when he gets away
1 *warrant* assure

2nd MERCHANT
If you could ship him away, 'twere excellent.
3rd MERCHANT
To Zant, or to Aleppo?
PEREGRINE Yes, and ha'his
Adventures put i'the *Book of Voyages*, 5
And his gulled story registered, for truth?
Well, gentlemen, when I am in, a while,
And that you think us warm in our discourse,
Know your approaches.
1st MERCHANT Trust it to our care.
[*Exeunt* MERCHANTS]

[*Enter* WAITING WOMAN]

PEREGRINE
Save you, fair lady. Is Sir Pol within? 10
WOMAN
I do not know, sir.
PEREGRINE Pray you, say unto him,
Here is a merchant, upon earnest business,
Desires to speak with him.
WOMAN I will see, sir.
PEREGRINE Pray you.
[*Exit* WOMAN]
I see, the family is all female, here.

[*Enter* WAITING WOMAN]

WOMAN
He says, sir, he has weighty affairs of state, 15
That now require him whole—some other time
You may possess him.
PEREGRINE Pray you, may again,
If those require him whole, these will exact him,

4 *Zant* Zante, one of the Ionian islands, and a Venetian possession at the time
5 *Book of Voyages* Hakluyt's *Principal Navigations* was published in its enlarged form in 1598–1600, but there were other books of voyages too
6 *gulled story* 'the story of his gulling'
9 *Know . . . approaches* get ready to enter (perhaps nautical jargon)
12 *earnest* weighty
16 *require . . . whole* require his whole attention
17 *possess him* have his company
18 *exact him* probably 'force him out', extract him from his study (see *OED*)

Whereof I bring him tidings. [*Exit* WOMAN] What might be
His grave affair of state, now? how to make 20
Bolognian sausages, here, in Venice, sparing
One o' th'ingredients.

[*Enter* WAITING WOMAN]

WOMAN Sir, he says, he knows
By your word, tidings, that you are no statesman,
And therefore, wills you stay.

PEREGRINE Sweet, pray you return him,
I have not read so many proclamations, 25
And studied them, for words, as he has done;
But—Here he deigns to come. [*Exit* WOMAN]

[*Enter* SIR POLITIC WOULD-BE]

SIR POLITIC Sir, I must crave
Your courteous pardon. There hath chanced, today,
Unkind disaster, 'twixt my lady, and me:
And I was penning my apology 30
To give her satisfaction, as you came, now.

PEREGRINE
Sir, I am grieved, I bring you worse disaster;
The gentleman, you met at the port, today,
That told you, he was newly arrived—

SIR POLITIC Ay, was
A fugitive-punk?

PEREGRINE No, sir, a spy, set on you: 35
And, he has made relation to the Senate,
That you professed to him, to have a plot,
To sell the state of Venice, to the Turk.

SIR POLITIC
O me!

PEREGRINE For which, warrants are signed by this time,

21 *Bolognian* sausages 'The mortadella of *Bologna* is still famous. Sir Thomas Gresham imported it to England from Rotterdam' (Herford and Simpson)
21 *sparing* leaving out
23 *tidings* Sir Politic's word is 'intelligence' (II. i, 68)
24 *return him* answer him
35 *punk* prostitute
36 *made relation* Peregrine now uses state language (see II.i, 96)
38 *to the Turk* see IV. i, 130

To apprehend you, and to search your study, 40
For papers—

SIR POLITIC Alas, sir. I have none, but notes,
Drawn out of play-books—

PEREGRINE All the better, sir.

SIR POLITIC
And some essays. What shall I do?

PEREGRINE Sir, best
Convey yourself into a sugar-chest,
Or, if you could lie round, a frail were rare: 45
And I could send you, aboard.

SIR POLITIC Sir, I but talked so,
For discourse sake, merely. *They knock without*

PEREGRINE Hark, they are there.

SIR POLITIC
I am a wretch, a wretch.

PEREGRINE What will you do, sir?
Ha'you ne'er a currant-butt to leap into?
They'll put you to the rack, you must be sudden. 50

SIR POLITIC
Sir, I have an engine—

3rd MERCHANT [*Off-stage*] Sir Politic Would-be?

2nd MERCHANT [*Off-stage*]
Where is he?

SIR POLITIC That I have thought upon, before time.

PEREGRINE
What is it?

SIR POLITIC —I shall ne'er endure the torture.—
Marry, it is, sir, of a tortoise-shell,
Fitted, for these extremities: 'pray you sir, help me. 55
Here, I've a place, sir, to put back my legs,—
Please you to lay it on, sir—with this cap,
And my black gloves, I'll lie, sir, like a tortoise,
Till they are gone.

PEREGRINE And, call you this an engine?

43 *essays* a literary form that Jonson despised (*Discoveries* 719–729)
44 *Convey* another Politic word (see II. i, 80)
45 *lie round* curl up
45 *frail* rush basket for figs
50 *sudden* quick
51 *engine* device, contrivance
54 *tortoise-shell* a feature of the Venetian market (see p. 164); the tortoise was a symbol of polity
55 *Fitted* F (Q Apted) suited

SIR POLITIC
Mine own device—good sir, bid my wife's women 60
To burn my papers.

[MERCHANTS] *rush in*

1st MERCHANT Where's he hid?
3rd MERCHANT We must,
And will, sure, find him.
2nd MERCHANT Which is his study?
1st MERCHANT What
Are you, sir?
PEREGRINE I'm a merchant, that came here
To look upon this tortoise.
3rd MERCHANT How?
1st MERCHANT St. Mark!
What beast is this?
PEREGRINE It is a fish.
2nd MERCHANT Come out, here. 65
PEREGRINE
Nay, you may strike him, sir, and tread upon him:
He'll bear a cart.
1st MERCHANT What, to run over him?
PEREGRINE Yes.
3rd MERCHANT
Let's jump upon him.
2nd MERCHANT Can he not go?
PEREGRINE He creeps, sir.
1st MERCHANT
Let's see him creep. [*Prods him*]
PEREGRINE No, good sir, you will hurt him.
2nd MERCHANT
Heart, I'll see him creep; or prick his guts. 70
3rd MERCHANT
Come out, here.
PEREGRINE Pray you sir. [*To* SIR POLITIC] Creep a little!
1st MERCHANT Forth!
2nd MERCHANT
Yet further.

60 *device* invention (of own devising)
61 s.d. Folio reads *They rush in.*
61 *burn my papers* Peregrine must tell the woman to do this as the merchants rush in and look round; the 'funeral' alluded to in line 76 may be visible to the audience from the gallery or an inner room

PEREGRINE Good sir! [*To* SIR POLITIC] Creep!
2nd MERCHANT We'll see his legs.

They pull off the shell and discover him

3rd MERCHANT
God's so—, he has garters!
1st MERCHANT Ay, and gloves!
2nd MERCHANT Is this
Your fearful tortoise?
PEREGRINE [*Throwing off his disguise*] Now, Sir Pol, we are even;
For your next project, I shall be prepared: 75
I am sorry for the funeral of your notes, sir.
1st MERCHANT
'Twere a rare motion, to be seen in Fleet Street!
2nd MERCHANT
Ay, i'the term.
1st MERCHANT Or Smithfield, in the fair.
3rd MERCHANT
Methinks, 'tis but a melancholic sight!
PEREGRINE
Farewell, most politic tortoise.
[*Exeunt* PEREGRINE, MERCHANTS]

[*Enter* WAITING WOMAN]

SIR POLITIC Where's my lady? 80
Knows she of this?
WOMAN I know not, sir.
SIR POLITIC Enquire. [*Exit* WOMAN]
O, I shall be the fable of all feasts;
The freight of the *gazetti*; ship-boys' tale;
And, which is worst, even talk for ordinaries.

[*Enter* WAITING WOMAN]

WOMAN
My lady's come most melancholic, home, 85
And says, sir, she will straight to sea, for physic.

73 *God's so—* see II. vi, 59n.
77 *motion* puppet-show
78 *term* the law term, when the lawyers of the Inns of Court were in residence and their clients in town
78 *Smithfield* site of Bartholomew Fair; Jonson's *Bartholomew Fair* features a puppet-show
83 *freight . . . gazetti* i.e. carried by the news-sheets
84 *ordinary* tavern (see II. i, 76n.)
86 *physic* medical treatment, recuperation

SIR POLITIC
And I, to shun, this place, and clime for ever;
Creeping, with house, on back: and think it well,
To shrink my poor head, in my politic shell.

Act V, Scene v

[VOLPONE's *House*]

[*Enter*] VOLPONE, MOSCA; *the first, in the habit of a Commendatore: the other, of a Clarissimo.*

VOLPONE
Am I then like him?
MOSCA
O, sir, you are he:
No man can sever you.
VOLPONE
Good.
MOSCA
But, what am I?
VOLPONE
'Fore heaven, a brave *clarissimo*, thou becom'st it!
Pity, thou wert not born one.
MOSCA
If I hold
My made one, 'twill be well.
VOLPONE
I'll go, and see 5
What news, first, at the court. [*Exit* VOLPONE]
MOSCA
Do so. My Fox
Is out on his hole, and, ere he shall re-enter,
I'll make him languish in his borrowed case,
Except he come to composition, with me:
Androgyno, Castrone, Nano!

[*Enter* ANDROGYNO, CASTRONE, NANO]

ALL
Here. 10
MOSCA
Go recreate yourselves, abroad; go, sport. [*Exeunt the three*]

s.d. *habit* Gifford describes the dress as 'a black stuff gown and a red cap with two gilt buttons in front.'
2 *sever* separate, distinguish
4 *hold* either 'keep up' or 'remain in' the assumed role; Mosca equivocates between modesty and guile
6–7 *Fox . . . hole* alluding to the boys' game, Fox-in-the-Hole; players hop, and strike each other with gloves and light thongs
8 *case* disguise 9 *Except* unless
9 *composition* agreement, compromise
11 *recreate* refresh, amuse 11 *abroad* outside

LX51

So, now I have the keys, and am possessed.
Since he will, needs, be dead, afore his time,
I'll bury him, or gain by him. I'm his heir:
And so will keep me, till he share at least. 15
To cozen him of all, were but a cheat
Well placed; no man would construe it a sin:
Let his sport pay for't, this is called the Fox-trap.

[*Exit* MOSCA]

Act V, Scene vi

[*A Street*]

[*Enter* CORBACCIO *and* CORVINO]

CORBACCIO
They say, the court is set.
CORVINO
We must maintain
Our first tale good, for both our reputations.
CORBACCIO
Why? mine's no tale: my son would, there, have killed me.
CORVINO
That's true, I had forgot: mine is, I am sure.
But, for your will, sir.
CORBACCIO
Ay, I'll come upon him, 5
For that, hereafter, now his patron's dead.

[*Enter* VOLPONE *disguised*]

VOLPONE
Signior Corvino! and Corbaccio! sir,
Much joy unto you.
CORVINO
Of what?
VOLPONE
The sudden good,
Dropped down upon you—
CORBACCIO
Where?
VOLPONE
And none knows how—
From old Volpone, sir.
CORBACCIO
Out, errant knave. 10
VOLPONE
Let not your too much wealth, sir, make you furious.

12 *possessed* in possession (but the word has its other potentials)
15 *keep me* remain
18 *Let . . . for't* 'Let his amusement compensate his loss', but 'sport' is also apt for the hunting and hunted fox
5 *come upon* 'make a demand or claim upon' (*OED*)
10 *errant* = arrant (see III. vii, 118n.)

CORBACCIO
Away, thou varlet.
VOLPONE Why sir?
CORBACCIO Dost thou mock me?
VOLPONE
You mock the world, sir, did you not change wills?
CORBACCIO
Out, harlot.
VOLPONE O! belike you are the man,
Signior Corvino? Faith, you carry it well; 15
You grow not mad withal: I love your spirit.
You are not over-leavened, with your fortune.
You should ha'some would swell, now, like a wine-fat,
With such an autumn—Did he gi' you all, sir?
CORVINO
Avoid, you rascal.
VOLPONE Troth, your wife has shown 20
Herself a very woman: but, you are well,
You need not care, you have a good estate,
To bear it out, sir: better by this chance.
Except Corbaccio have a share?
CORBACCIO Hence, varlet.
VOLPONE
You will not be aknown, sir: why, 'tis wise. 25
Thus do all gamesters, at all games, dissemble.
No man will seem to win. [*Exeunt* CORBACCIO, CORVINO]
Here, comes my vulture,
Heaving his beak up i'the air, and snuffing.

Act V, Scene vii

[*Enter* VOLTORE *to* VOLPONE]

VOLTORE
Outstripped thus, by a parasite? a slave?

13 *mock the world* 'are laughing at everyone'
13 *change* exchange
17 *over-leavened* puffed up (as with too much yeast)
18 *You . . . swell* 'You'd have some swelling . . .'
18 *wine-fat* wine-vat
19 *autumn* i.e. harvest
20 *Avoid* be gone!
21 *a very woman* a woman indeed
23 *bear it out* carry it off
25 *aknown* acknowledged (to be the heir)

Would run on errands? and make legs, for crumbs?
Well, what I'll do—

VOLPONE The court stays for your worship.
I e'en rejoice, sir, at your worship's happiness,
And that it fell into so learned hands, 5
That understand the fingering.—

VOLTORE What do you mean?

VOLPONE
I mean to be a suitor to your worship,
For the small tenement, out of reparations;
That, at the end of your long row of houses,
By the Piscaria: it was, in Volpone's time, 10
Your predecessor, ere he grew diseased,
A handsome, pretty, customed, bawdy-house,
As any was in Venice (none dispraised)
But fell with him; his body, and that house
Decayed, together.

VOLTORE Come, sir, leave your prating. 15

VOLPONE
Why, if your worship give me but your hand,
That I may ha'the refusal; I have done.
'Tis a mere toy to you, sir; candle-rents:
As your learn'd worship knows—

VOLTORE What do I know?

VOLPONE
Marry, no end of your wealth, sir, God decrease it! 20

VOLTORE
Mistaking knave! what, mock'st thou my misfortune?

VOLPONE
His blessing on your heart, sir, would 'twere more.
[*Exit* VOLTORE]
—Now, to my first, again; at the next corner.
[*Watches, apart*]

2 *make legs* bow and scrape
3 *stays* waits
8 *tenement* house
8 *reparations* repair(s)
10 *Piscaria* fish-market
12 *customed* well patronised
17 *refusal* i.e. 'first refusal'
18 *candle-rents* rents from deteriorating property (self-consuming, like candles)
20 *decrease* a calculated Dogberryism for 'increase'; hence the double force of Voltore's response 'Mistaking knave'

Act V, Scene viii

[*Enter*] CORBACCIO, CORVINO, (MOSCA *passant*)

CORBACCIO
See, in our habit! see the impudent varlet!
CORVINO
That I could shoot mine eyes at him, like gun-stones!
VOLPONE
But, is this true, sir, of the parasite?
CORBACCIO
Again, t'afflict us? monster!
VOLPONE In good faith, sir,
I'm heartily grieved, a beard of your grave length 5
Should be so over-reached. I never brooked
That parasite's hair, methought his nose should cozen:
There still was somewhat, in his look, did promise
The bane of a *clarissimo*.
CORBACCIO Knave—
VOLPONE Methinks,
Yet you, that are so traded i'the world, 10
A witty merchant, the fine bird, Corvino,
That have such moral emblems on your name,
Should not have sung your shame; and dropped your cheese:
To let the Fox laugh at your emptiness.
CORVINO
Sirrah, you think, the privilege of the place, 15
And your red saucy cap, that seems, to me,
Nailed to your jolt-head, with those two chequeens,
Can warrant your abuses; come you, hither:
You shall perceive, sir, I dare beat you. Approach.

s.d. MOSCA *passant* i.e. crosses the stage in his role of *clarissimo*
2 *gun-stones* stone cannon-shot
5 *beard . . . length* 'one so old and wise', but probably literal too
9 *bane* ruin, destruction
10 *traded* experienced
12 *moral emblems* Corvino's name recalls the crow that dropped its cheese to sing to the fox; see p. 157
14 *emptiness* i.e. of belly and of head
15 *place* station, rank (as a commendatore)
17 *jolt-head* block-head
17 *chequeens* i.e. the coin-like buttons on his hat (see V. v, s.d. note)
18 *warrant* sanction, protect by official authority

VOLPONE
No haste, sir, I do know your valour, well: 20
Since you durst publish what you are, sir.
CORVINO Tarry,
I'd speak, with you.
VOLPONE Sir, sir, another time—
CORVINO
Nay, now.
VOLPONE O God, sir! I were a wise man,
Would stand the fury of a distracted cuckold.

Mosca walks by 'em

CORBACCIO
What! come again?
VOLPONE Upon 'em, Mosca; save me! 25
CORBACCIO
The air's infected, where he breathes.
CORVINO Let's fly him.
VOLPONE
Excellent basilisk! turn upon the vulture.

Act V, Scene ix

[*Enter* VOLTORE]

VOLTORE
Well, flesh-fly, it is summer with you, now;
Your winter will come on.
MOSCA Good advocate,
Pray thee, not rail, nor threaten out of place, thus;
Thou'lt make a solecism, as madam says.
Get you a biggin more: your brain breaks loose. 5
VOLTORE
Well, sir.
VOLPONE Would you ha' me beat the insolent slave?
Throw dirt, upon his first good clothes?
VOLTORE This same
Is, doubtless, some familiar!
VOLPONE Sir, the court

24 *stand* withstand
27 *basilisk* or cockatrice, a fabulous reptile hatched by a serpent from a cock's egg and capable of killing by its glance
1 *flesh-fly* a blow-fly, the meaning of 'Mosca'
4 *solecism* see IV. ii, 43 and note
5 *biggin* lawyer's cap or coif
8 *familiar* i.e. 'some fellow of the same household'

In troth, stays for you. I am mad, a mule,
That never read Justinian, should get up, 10
And ride an advocate. Had you no quirk,
To avoid gullage, sir, by such a creature?
I hope you do but jest; he has not done't:
This's but confederacy, to blind the rest.
You are the heir?

VOLTORE A strange, officious, 15
Troublesome knave! thou dost torment me.

VOLPONE I know—
It cannot be, sir, that you should be cozened;
'Tis not within the wit of man, to do it:
You are so wise, so prudent—and, 'tis fit,
That wealth, and wisdom still, should go together. 20

x 32

Act V, Scene x

[*The Scrutineo*]

[*Enter*] *Four* AVOCATORI, NOTARIO, COMMENDATORI, BONARIO, CELIA, CORBACCIO, CORVINO.

1st AVOCATORE
Are all the parties, here?

NOTARIO All, but the advocate.

2nd AVOCATORE
And, here he comes.

[*Enter* VOLTORE, *with* VOLPONE *disguised*]

1st AVOCATORE Then bring 'em forth to sentence.

VOLTORE
O, my most honoured fathers, let your mercy
Once win upon your justice, to forgive—
I am distracted—

9 *mad* furious (that)
9 *mule* mules were customarily ridden by lawyers
10 *Justinian* i.e. the *Corpus Jurus Civilis*, the Roman code of law compiled under the direction of Justinian I
11 *quirk* trick
12 *gullage* being gulled
14 *confederacy* i.e. between Mosca and Voltore
2 s.p. 1st AVOCATORE ed. (F AVO. Q AVOC.); it is possible that F intends AVOCATORI, and that they speak together; likewise the ascription at line 20 below
4 *win upon* overcome

VOLPONE [*Aside*] What will he do, now?
VOLTORE O, 5
I know not which t'address myself to, first,
Whether your fatherhoods, or these innocents—
CORVINO [*Aside*]
Will he betray himself?
VOLTORE Whom, equally,
I have abused, out of most covetous ends—
CORVINO [*To* CORBACCIO]
The man is mad!
CORBACCIO What's that?
CORVINO He is possessed. 10
VOLTORE
For which, now struck in conscience, here I prostrate
Myself, at your offended feet, for pardon.
1st and 2nd AVOCATORI
Arise!
CELIA O heaven, how just thou art?
VOLPONE [*Aside*] I'm caught
I'mine own noose—
CORVINO [*To* CORBACCIO] Be constant, sir, nought now
Can help, but impudence.
1st AVOCATORE Speak forward.
COMMENDATORE Silence! 15
VOLTORE
It is not passion in me, reverend fathers,
But only conscience, conscience, my good sires,
That makes me, now, tell truth. That parasite,
That knave hath been the instrument of all.
2nd AVOCATORE
Where is that knave? fetch him!
VOLPONE I go. [*Exit* VOLPONE]
CORVINO Grave fathers, 20
This man's distracted; he confessed it, now:
For, hoping to be old Volpone's heir,
Who now is dead—
3rd AVOCATORE How?

9 *ends* purposes, motives
10 *possessed* i.e. of a devil
14 *constant* firm, consistent
15 *impudence* unblushing effrontery
16 *passion* frenzy
20 s.p. 2nd AVOCATORE ed. (F AVO. Q AVOC.) see note line 2 above
21 *now* just now (line 5 above)

2nd AVOCATORE Is Volpone dead?

CORVINO

Dead since, grave fathers—

BONARIO O, sure vengeance!

1st AVOCATORE Stay,

Then, he was no deceiver?

VOLTORE O no, none: 25

The parasite, grave fathers—

CORVINO He does speak,

Out of mere envy, 'cause the servant's made
The thing, he gaped for; please your fatherhoods,
This is the truth: though, I'll not justify
The other, but he may be some-deal faulty. 30

VOLTORE

Ay, to your hopes, as well as mine, Corvino:
But I'll use modesty. Pleaseth your wisdoms
To view these certain notes, and but confer them;

[*Gives them papers*]

As I hope favour, they shall speak clear truth.

CORVINO

The devil has entered him!

BONARIO Or bides in you. 35

4th AVOCATORE

We have done ill, by a public officer
To send for him, if he be heir.

2nd AVOCATORE For whom?

4th AVOCATORE

Him, that they call the parasite.

3rd AVOCATORE 'Tis true;

He is a man, of great estate, now left.

4th AVOCATORE

Go you, and learn his name; and say, the court 40

27 *made* achieved, grabbed
28 *gaped for* hungered after; a noticeable word in *Volpone*—see I. ii, 97n., I. iv, 42, V. ii, 74
30 *but he may* 'he may yet'
30 *some-deal* F (Q somewhere)
32 *modesty* moderation
33 *certain* 'particular' or perhaps 'reliable'
33 *confer* either 'compare' or 'consult together about'
36 *public officer* describing the status of Volpone as commendatore (line 20); now the Notario is sent (as indicated at V. xii, 13); F and Q have a comma after 'officer', which might add to the bewilderment expressed by the 2nd Avocatore's question

Entreats his presence, here; but, to the clearing
Of some few doubts. [*Exit* NOTARIO]

2nd AVOCATORE This same's a labyrinth!

1st AVOCATORE
Stand you unto your first report?

CORVINO My state,
My life, my fame—

BONARIO [*Aside*] Where is it?

CORVINO Are at the stake.

1st AVOCATORE
Is yours so too?

CORBACCIO The advocate's a knave: 45
And has a forked tongue—

2nd AVOCATORE Speak to the point.

CORBACCIO
So is the parasite, too.

1st AVOCATORE This is confusion.

VOLTORE
I do beseech your fatherhoods, read but those.

CORVINO
And credit nothing, the false spirit hath writ:
It cannot be, but he is possessed, grave fathers. 50

Act V, Scene xi

[*A Street*]

[*Enter*] VOLPONE

VOLPONE
To make a snare, for mine own neck! and run
My head into it, wilfully! with laughter!
When I had newly scaped, was free, and clear!
Out of mere wantonness! O, the dull devil
Was in this brain of mine, when I devised it; 5
And Mosca gave it second: he must now
Help to sear up this vein, or we bleed dead.

[*Enter* NANO, ANDROGYNO, CASTRONE]

LX 33

43 *state* estate
44 *Are . . . stake* 'are all staked on the truth of what I have said'
4 *dull devil* 'devil of stupidity'
6 *gave it second* seconded it
7 *sear* cauterise, stem blood with hot iron

How now! who let you loose? whither go you, now?
What? to buy ginger-bread? or to drown kitlings?

NANO
Sir, master Mosca called us out of doors. 10
And bid us all go play, and took the keys.

ANDROGYNO
Yes.

VOLPONE
Did master Mosca take the keys? why, so!
I am farther in. These are my fine conceits!
I must be merry, with a mischief to me!
What a vile wretch was I, that could not bear 15
My fortune soberly? I must ha' my crotchets!
And my conundrums! well, go you, and seek him:
His meaning may be truer, than my fear.
Bid him, he straight come to me, to the court;
Thither will I, and, if't be possible, 20
Unscrew my advocate, upon new hopes:
When I provoked him, then I lost myself.

Act V, Scene xii

[*The Scrutineo*]

[*Four* AVOCATORI, NOTARIO, VOLTORE, BONARIO, CELIA, CORBACCIO, CORVINO, COMMENDATORI]

1st AVOCATORE [*With* VOLTORE'*s notes*]
These things can ne'er be reconciled. He, here,
Professeth, that the gentleman was wronged;
And that the gentlewoman was brought thither,
Forced by her husband: and there left.

VOLTORE
Most true.

9 *buy . . . kitlings* presumably the pastimes of self-indulgent and malicious children
13 *conceits* notions, schemes
14 *with . . . to me* either reflective, 'with this mischievous result', or imprecatory, 'a mischief take me!'
16 *fortune* i.e. good fortune in surviving the court action, or perhaps 'wealth'
16 *crotchets* whimsical fancies, perverse conceits (*OED*)
17 *conundrums* whims, crotchets
21 *Unscrew* i.e. 'dislodge him from his present course'; or perhaps 'unwind him' as if he were a loaded cross-bow
21 *upon* used to indicate manner—'in' or 'by'

CELIA

How ready is heaven to those, that pray!

1st AVOCATORE But, that 5

Volpone would have ravished her, he holds
Utterly false; knowing his impotence.

CORVINO

Grave fathers, he is possessed; again, I say,
Possessed: nay, if there be possession,
And obsession, he has both.

3rd AVOCATORE Here comes our officer. 10

[*Enter* VOLPONE, *disguised*]

VOLPONE

The parasite will straight be here, grave fathers.

4th AVOCATORE

You might invent some other name, sir varlet.

3rd AVOCATORE

Did not the notary meet him?

VOLPONE Not that I know.

4th AVOCATORE

His coming will clear all.

2nd AVOCATORE Yet it is misty.

VOLTORE

May't please your fatherhoods—

VOLPONE *whispers* [*to*] *the Advocate*

VOLPONE Sir, the parasite 15

Willed me to tell you, that his master lives;
That you are still the man; your hopes, the same;
And this was, only a jest—

VOLTORE How?

VOLPONE Sir, to try

If you were firm, and how you stood affected.

VOLTORE

Art sure he lives?

VOLPONE Do I live, sir?

VOLTORE O me! 20

I was too violent.

10 *obsession* 'actuation by the devil or an evil spirit from without' (*OED*) 12 *invent* find
12 *varlet* menial or knave (here used to slight the commendatore)
19 *how . . . affected* 'which way you were inclined', 'how you would feel and act'
20 *Do . . . sir?* Volpone evidently discloses his identity to Voltore, perhaps by showing his red hair, or a signet ring

VOLPONE Sir, you may redeem it—
They said, you were possessed; fall down, and seem so:
I'll help to make it good. VOLTORE *falls*
God bless the man!
[*Aside*] Stop your wind hard, and swell—See, see, see, see!
He vomits crooked pins! his eyes are set, 25
Like a dead hare's, hung in a poulter's shop!
His mouth's running away! do you see, signior?
Now, 'tis in his belly.

CORVINO Ay, the devil!

VOLPONE
Now, in his throat.

CORVINO Ay, I perceive it plain.

VOLPONE
'Twill out, 'twill out; stand clear. See, where it flies! 30
In shape of a blue toad, with a bat's wings!
Do not you see it, sir?

CORBACCIO What? I think I do.

CORVINO
'Tis too manifest.

VOLPONE Look! he comes t'himself!

VOLTORE
Where am I?

VOLPONE Take good heart, the worst is past, sir.
You are dispossessed.

1st AVOCATORE What accident is this? 35

2nd AVOCATORE
Sudden, and full of wonder!

3rd AVOCATORE If he were
Possessed, as it appears, all this is nothing.

CORVINO
He has been, often, subject to these fits.

1st AVOCATORE
Show him that writing, do you know it, sir?

VOLPONE [*Aside to* VOLTORE]
Deny it, sir, forswear it, know it not. 40

24 *Stop your wind* hold your breath
25–31 *crooked pins . . . bat's wings* imitated from details in accounts of contemporary impostures (see p. 165)
26 *poulter's* poulterers
27 *running away* twisting from one side to the other (see p. 166)

VOLTORE
Yes, I do know it well, it is my hand:
But all, that it contains, is false.
BONARIO O practice!
2nd AVOCATORE
What maze is this!
1st AVOCATORE Is he not guilty, then,
Whom you, there, name the parasite?
VOLTORE Grave fathers,
No more than, his good patron, old Volpone. 45
4th AVOCATORE
Why, he is dead?
VOLTORE O no, my honoured fathers.
He lives—
1st AVOCATORE How! lives?
VOLTORE Lives.
2nd AVOCATORE This is subtler yet!
3rd AVOCATORE
You said he was dead!
VOLTORE Never.
3rd AVOCATORE [*To* CORVINO] You said so!
CORVINO I heard so.
4th AVOCATORE
Here comes the gentleman, make him way.

[*Enter* MOSCA *as clarissimo*]

3rd AVOCATORE A stool!
4th AVOCATORE [*Aside*]
A proper man! and were Volpone dead, 50
A fit match for my daughter.
3rd AVOCATORE Give him way.
VOLPONE [*Aside to* MOSCA]
Mosca, I was almost lost, the advocate
Had betrayed all; but, now, it is recovered:
All's o'the hinge again—say, I am living.
MOSCA
What busy knave is this! most reverend fathers, 55
I sooner, had attended your grave pleasures,

41 *hand* handwriting
47 *subtler* more elusive and bewildering
50 *proper* handsome
53 *recovered* got back again; covered up again
54 *o' the hinge* running smoothly, no longer unhinged (o' = on)
55 *busy* officious

But that my order, for the funeral
Of my dear patron did require me—
VOLPONE [*Aside*] Mosca!
MOSCA
Whom I intend to bury, like a gentleman.
VOLPONE [*Aside*]
Aye, quick, and cozen me of all.
2nd AVOCATORE Still stranger! 60
More intricate!
1st AVOCATORE And come about again!
4th AVOCATORE [*Aside*]
It is a match, my daughter is bestowed.
MOSCA [*Aside to* VOLPONE]
Will you give me half?
VOLPONE [*Aside to* MOSCA] First, I'll be hanged.
MOSCA [*Aside to* VOLPONE] I know,
Your voice is good, cry not so loud.
1st AVOCATORE Demand
The advocate. Sir, did you not affirm, 65
Volpone was alive?
VOLPONE Yes, and he is;
This gent'man told me so. [*Aside to* MOSCA] Thou shalt have half.
MOSCA
Whose drunkard is this same? speak some that know him:
I never saw his face. [*Aside to* VOLPONE] I cannot now
Afford it you so cheap.
VOLPONE [*Aside to* MOSCA] No?
1st AVOCATORE What say you? 70
VOLTORE
The officer told me.
VOLPONE I did, grave fathers,
And will maintain, he lives, with mine own life.
And, that this creature told me. [*Aside*] I was born
With all good stars my enemies.
MOSCA Most grave fathers,
If such an insolence, as this, must pass 75
Upon me, I am silent: 'twas not this,
For which you sent, I hope.
2nd AVOCATORE Take him away.

60 *quick* alive
61 *come about* turned round, reversed
64 *cry* shout 64 *Demand* ask
74 *good* propitious 75 *pass* be allowed

VOLPONE [*Aside*]
Mosca!

3rd AVOCATORE
Let him be whipped,—

VOLPONE [*Aside*] Wilt thou betray me?
Cozen me?

3rd AVOCATORE And taught to bear himself
Toward a person of his rank.

4th AVOCATORE Away. [VOLPONE *is seized*] 80

MOSCA
I humbly thank your fatherhoods.

VOLPONE [*Aside*] Soft, soft: whipped?
And lose all that I have? if I confess,
It cannot be much more.

4th AVOCATORE [*To* MOSCA] Sir, are you married?

VOLPONE
They'll be allied, anon; I must be resolute:
He puts off his disguise
The Fox shall, here, uncase.

LX 35

MOSCA Patron!

VOLPONE Nay, now, 85
My ruins shall not come alone; your match
I'll hinder sure: my substance shall not glue you,
Nor screw you, into a family.

MOSCA Why, patron!

VOLPONE
I am Volpone, and this is my knave;
This, his own knave; this, avarice's fool; 90
This, a chimera of wittol, fool, and knave;
And, reverend fathers, since we all can hope
Nought, but a sentence, let's not now despair it.
You hear me brief.

84 *allied* i.e. by a marriage bargain
84 *anon* in a moment
85 *uncase* remove disguise, perhaps with a suggestion of the fox breaking cover
85 *Patron*! Mosca is apparently startled back into his servile role
87 *glue* suggests a parasitic attachment
88 *screw* suggests a tortuous one
89 *knave* menial; rogue
90 *fool* dupe
91 *chimera* mythical beast with a lion-head, goat-body and serpent-tail; hence a triple monster
91 *wittol* conniving cuckold
93 *let's . . . it* 'let us not despair for want of a sentence'

CORVINO May it please your fatherhoods—
COMMENDATORE Silence!
1st AVOCATORE
The knot is now undone, by miracle! 95
2nd AVOCATORE
Nothing can be more clear.
3rd AVOCATORE Or can more prove
These innocent.
1st AVOCATORE Give 'em their liberty.
BONARIO
Heaven could not, long, let such gross crimes be hid.
2nd AVOCATORE
If this be held the highway to get riches,
May I be poor.
3rd AVOCATORE This's not the gain, but torment. 100
1st AVOCATORE
These possess wealth, as sick men possess fevers,
Which, trulier, may be said to possess them.
2nd AVOCATORE
Disrobe that parasite.
CORVINO, MOSCA Most honoured fathers—
1st AVOCATORE
Can you plead ought to stay the course of justice?
If you can, speak.
CORVINO, VOLTORE We beg favour.
CELIA And mercy. 105
1st AVOCATORE
You hurt your innocence, suing for the guilty.
Stand forth; and first, the parasite. You appear
T'have been the chiefest minister, if not plotter,
In all these lewd impostures; and now, lastly,
Have, with your impudence, abused the court, 110
And habit of a gentleman of Venice,
Being a fellow of no birth, or blood:
For which, our sentence is, first thou be whipped;
Then live perpetual prisoner in our gallies.
VOLPONE
I thank you, for him.
MOSCA Bane to thy woolvish nature. 115

100 *This's* i.e. riches 108 *minister* agent, instrument
109 *lewd* wicked, base
115 s.p. VOLPONE ed. (FQ VOLT.) Gifford recognised the connection with line 81 where Mosca thanks the court for Volpone's sentence 115 *Bane* death

1st AVOCATORE

Deliver him to the Saffi. [MOSCA *is led off*] Thou, Volpone,
By blood, and rank a gentleman, canst not fall
Under like censure; but our judgement on thee
Is, that thy substance all be straight confiscate
To the hospital, of the *Incurabili*: 120
And, since the most was gotten by imposture,
By feigning lame, gout, palsy, and such diseases,
Thou art to lie in prison, cramped with irons,
Till thou be'st sick, and lame indeed. Remove him.

VOLPONE

This is called mortifying of a fox. [VOLPONE *is led off*] 125

1st AVOCATORE

Thou, Voltore, to take away the scandal
Thou hast given all worthy men, of thy profession,
Art banished from their fellowship, and our state.
Corbaccio!—bring him near. We here possess
Thy son, of all thy state; and confine thee 130
To the monastery of *San Spirito*:
Where, since thou knew'st not how to live well here,
Thou shalt be learn'd to die well.

CORBACCIO Ha! what said he?

COMMENDATORE

You shall know anon, sir.

1st AVOCATORE Thou, Corvino, shalt
Be straight embarked from thine own house, and rowed 135
Round about Venice, through the Grand Canal,
Wearing a cap, with fair, long ass's ears,
Instead of horns: and, so to mount, a paper
Pinned on thy breast, to the *berlino*—

CORVINO Yes,
And, have mine eyes beat out with stinking fish, 140

116 *Saffi* bailiffs (see III.viii, 16n.)
120 *Incurabili* the Hospital of Incurables was founded in Venice in 1522 for the treatment of venereal disease; the punishment is therefore particularly appropriate
125 *mortifying* several senses are relevant: humiliating; rendering dead to the world and the flesh by spiritual discipline; hanging game to make it tender
131 *San Spirito* the monastery of the Holy Spirit stood on the Giudecca canal
136 *Canal* the FQ *canale* probably indicates Italian pronunciation, as the English word was not then used in this sense
139 *berlino* pillory

Bruised fruit, and rotten eggs—'Tis well. I'm glad,
I shall not see my shame, yet.

1st AVOCATORE And to expiate
Thy wrongs done to thy wife, thou art to send her
Home, to her father, with her dowry trebled:
And these are all your judgements—

ALL Honoured fathers. 145

1st AVOCATORE
Which may not be revoked. Now, you begin,
When crimes are done, and past, and to be punished,
To think what your crimes are: away with them!
Let all, that see these vices thus rewarded,
Take heart, and love to study 'em. Mischiefs feed 150
Like beasts, till they be fat, and then they bleed. [*Exeunt*]

VOLPONE

[*To speak the Epilogue*]

VOLPONE
The seasoning of a play is the applause.
Now, though the Fox be punished by the laws,
He, yet, doth hope there is no suffering due,
For any fact, which he hath done 'gainst you; 155
If there be, censure him: here he, doubtful, stands.
If not, fare jovially, and clap your hands.

THE END

155 *fact* crime (as in the legal phrase 'after the fact')

APPENDIX I

ANALOGUES AND DOCUMENTS

AS INDICATED in the Introduction and notes, the play has no one specific source but is nevertheless intricately connected with the literature and drama of the past. The following extracts are intended in part to suggest those connections and in part to supply background material relating to early seventeenth-century Venice.

LEGACY HUNTING

Horace, *Satires*, *II.v*, *45–57* [Loeb Classical Library, 1929]

Si cui praeterea validus male filius in re
praeclara sublatus aletur, ne manifestum
caelibis obsequium nudet te, leniter in spem
adrepe officiosus, ut et scribare secundus
heres et, si quis casus puerum egerit Orco,
in vacuum venias: perraro haec alea fallit.
Qui testamentum tradet tibi cumque legendum,
abnuere et tabulas a te removere memento,
sic tamen, ut limis rapias, quid prima secundo
cera velit versu; solus multisne coheres,
veloci percurre oculo. plerumque recoctus
scriba ex quinqueviro corvum deludet hiantem,
captatorque dabit risus Nasica Corano.

Again, if one with a fine fortune rears a sickly son whom he has taken up, then for fear lest open devotion to a childless man betray you, by your attentions worm your way to the hope that you may be named as second heir, and if some chance send the child to his grave, you may pass into his place. Seldom does this game fail.

Suppose someone gives you his will to read, be sure to decline and push the tablets from you; yet in such a way that with a side glance you may catch the substance of the second line on the first page. Swiftly run your eye across to see whether you are sole heir or share with others. Quite often a constable, new-boiled into a clerk, will dupe the gaping raven, and Nasica the fortune-hunter will make sport for Coranus.

Lucian, Dialogues of the Dead V [translated H. Williams, 1913]

Pluto and Hermes

Pluto. You know that old man, I mean the very aged and infirm fellow, the rich Eukrates, who has no children, but fifty thousand legacy-hunters?

Hermes. Yes, you speak of the Sikyonian. What then?

Pluto. Well, let him live on, Hermes; to the ninety years he has already reached dealing out so many again, and, if, at least, it were possible, even yet more. But as for those fawning flatterers of his, the young Charinus, and Damon, and the rest, drag them all down here, one after the other, the whole lot of them.

Hermes. Such a proceeding would appear strange.

Pluto. Not at all, but exceedingly just. For what wrong have they suffered that they pray for his death, or, although no way related, why do they lay claim to his money? But what of all things is most abominable is, that though they entertain such wishes, they yet court and fawn upon him in public; and, when he is ill, their designs are very evident to all; but, all the same, they engage to offer a sacrifice if he should get better; and, altogether, the fawning of these gentlemen is of a somewhat subtle and complicated character. So let the one remain untouched by death, and let the others go off before him, while vainly gaping *in affected admiration*.

Hermes. They will suffer a ridiculous fate, rascals that they are. But he, indeed, charmingly cheats and buoys them up with vain hopes exceedingly; and, in a word, while always appearing like a corpse, he has far more strength than the young men. They, however, already have divided out the legacy among themselves, and are living upon it, promising to themselves a happy time of it.

Pluto. Therefore, let him put off his old age and renew his youth like Iolaus; but as for them, in the midst of their hopes, leaving behind them the wealth they have been dreaming of, let them come *here* this moment, miserable wretches dying miserably.

Hermes. Have no anxiety, Pluto; for I will go after them for you at once, one by one in their order. There are seven of them, I believe.

Pluto. Drag them down. The old fellow shall follow each of them to the tomb, while he himself, from being aged, shall again be in the prime of youth.

THE AFFLICTIONS OF AGE

Juvenal, Satire X 188–208, 217–239 [Loeb Classical Library, 1940]

'Da spatium vitae, multos da, Iuppiter, annos':
hoc recto vultu, solum hoc, et pallidus optas.
sed quam continuis et quantis longa senectus
plena malis! deformem et taetrum ante omnia vultum
dissimilemque sui, deformem pro cute pellem
pendentisque genas et talis aspice rugas
quales, umbriferos ubi pandit Thabraca saltus,
in vetula scalpit iam mater simia bucca.
plurima sunt iuvenum discrimina; pulchrior ille
hoc atque ille alio, multum hic robustior illo:
una senum facies. cum voce trementia membra
et iam leve caput madidique infantia nasi,
frangendus misero gingiva panis inermi;
usque adeo gravis uxori natisque sibique,
ut captatori moveat fastidia Cosso.
non eadem vini atque cibi torpente palato
gaudia. nam coitus iam longa oblivio, vel si
coneris, iacet exiguus cum ramice nervus
et quamvis tota palpetur nocte, iacebit.
anne aliquid sperare potest haec inguinis aegri
canities? quid quod merito suspecta libido est
quae venerem adfectat sine viribus?

Praeterea minimus gelido iam in corpore sanguis
febre calet sola, circumsilit agmine facto
morborum omne genus, quorum si nomina quaeras,
promptius expediam quot amaverit Oppia moechos,
quot Themison aegros autumno occiderit uno,
quot Basilus socios, quot circumscripserit Hirrus
pupillos; quot longa viros exorbeat uno
Maura die, quot discipulos inclinet Hamillus;
percurram citius quot villas possideat nunc
quo tondente gravis iuveni mihi barba sonabat.
ille umero, hic lumbis, hic coxa debilis; ambos
perdidit ille oculos et luscis invidet; huius
pallida labra cibum accipiunt digitis alienis,
ipse ad conspectum cenae diducere rictum
suetus hiat tantum ceu pullus hirundinis, ad quem
ore volat pleno mater ieiuna. sed omni
membrorum damno maior dementia, quae nec
nomina servorum nec vultum agnoscit amici
cum quo praeterita cenavit nocte, nec illos

quos genuit, quos eduxit. nam codice saevo
heredes vetat esse suos, bona tota feruntur
ad Phialen; tantum artificis valet halitus oris
quod steterat multis in carcere fornicis annis.

'Give me length of days, give me many years, O Jupiter!' Such is your one and only prayer, in days of strength or of sickness; yet how great, how unceasing, are the miseries of long old age! Look first at the misshapen and ungainly face, so unlike its former self; see the unsightly hide that serves for skin; see the pendulous cheeks and the wrinkles like those which a matron baboon carves upon her aged jaws where Thabraca spreads her shaded glades. The young men differ in various ways: this man is handsomer than that, and he than another; one is far stronger than another: but old men all look alike. Their voices are as shaky as their limbs, their heads without hair, their noses drivelling as in childhood. Their bread, poor wretches, has to be munched by toothless gums; so offensive do they become to their wives, their children and themselves, that even the legacy-hunter, Cossus, turns from them in disgust. Their sluggish palate takes joy in wine or food no longer, and all pleasures of the flesh have been long ago forgotten. . . .

Besides all this, the little blood in his now chilly frame is never warm except with fever; diseases of every kind dance around him in a troop; if you ask of me their names, I could more readily tell you the number of Oppia's paramours, how many patients Themison killed in one autumn, how many partners were defrauded by Basilus, or wards by Hirrus, or pupils are corrupted by Hamillus, how many lovers tall Maura wears out in one day; I could sooner run over the number of villas now belonging to the barber under whose razor my stiff youthful beard used to grate. One suffers in the shoulder, another in the loins, a third in the hip; another has lost both eyes, and envies those who have one; another takes food into his pallid lips from someone else's fingers, while he whose jaws used to fly open at the sight of his dinner, now only gapes like the young of a swallow whose fasting mother flies to him with well-laden beak. But worse than any loss in body is the failing mind which forgets the names of slaves, and cannot recognise the face of the old friend who dined with him last night, nor those of the children whom he has begotten and brought up. Yes, by a cruel will he cuts off his own flesh and blood and leaves all his estate to Phiale—so potent was the breath of that alluring mouth which had plied its trade for so many years in her narrow archway.

THE VENETIAN SCENE [from Thomas Coryat, *Crudities* (1611, 1905)]

The Treasure of Saint Mark

Here they say is kept marveilous abundance of rich stones of exceeding worth, as Diamonds, Carbuncles, Emerauds, Chrysolites, Jacinths, and great pearles of admirable value: also three Unicorns hornes; an exceeding great Carbuncle which was bestowed upon the Senate by the Cardinall Grimannus, and a certaine Pitcher adorned with great variety of pretious stones, which Usumcassanes King of Persia bestowed upon the Signiory, with many other things of wonderful value.

Mountebanks

I hope it will not be esteemed for an impertinencie to my discourse, if I next speake of the Mountebanks of Venice, seeing amongst many other thinges that doe much famouse this Citie, these two sorts of people, namely the Cortezans and the Mountebanks are not the least: for although there are Mountebanks also in other Cities of Italy; yet because there is a greater concurse of them in Venice then else where, and that of the better sort and the most eloquent fellowes; and also for that there is a larger tolleration of them here then in other Cities (for in Rome, &c. they are restrained from certain matters as I have heard which are heere allowed them) therefore they use to name a Venetian Mountebanke κατ' ἐξοχην for the coryphaeus and principall Mountebanke of all Italy: neither doe I much doubt but that this treatise of them will be acceptable to some readers, as being a meere novelty never before heard of (I thinke) by thousands of our English Gallants. Surely the principall reason that hath induced me to make mention of them is, because when I was in Venice, they oftentimes ministred infinite pleasure unto me.

The principall place where they act, is the first part of Saint Marks street that reacheth betwixt the West front of S. Marks Church, and the opposite front of Saint Geminians Church. In which, twice a day, that is, in the morning and in the afternoone, you may see five or sixe severall stages erected for them: those that act upon the ground, even the foresaid Ciarlatans being of the poorer sort of them, stand most commonly in the second part of S. Marks, not far from the gate of the Dukes Palace. These Mountebanks at one end of their stage place their trunke, which is replenished with a world of new-fangled trumperies. After the whole rabble of them is gotten up to the stage, whereof some weare visards being disguised like fooles in a play, some that are women (for there are divers women also amongst them) are attyred with habits according to that person that they sustaine; after (I say) they are all upon the stage, the musicke begins. Sometimes vocall, sometimes instrumentall, and sometimes both together. This musicke is a preamble and introduction to the ensuing matter: in the meane time while the musicke playes, the principall Mountebanke which is the Captaine and ring-leader of all the rest, opens his truncke, and sets abroach his wares; after the musicke hath ceased, he maketh an oration to the audience of halfe an houre long, or almost an houre. Wherein he doth most hyperbolically extoll the vertue of his drugs and confections:

Laudat venales qui vult extrudere merces.

Though many of them are very counterfeit and false. Truly I often wondered at many of these naturall Orators. For they would tell their tales with such admirable volubility and plausible grace, even extempore, and seasoned with that singular variety of elegant jests and witty conceits, that they did often strike great admiration into strangers that never heard them before: and by how much the more eloquent these Naturalists are, by so much the greater audience they draw unto them, and the more ware they sell. After the chiefest Mountebankes first speech is ended, he delivereth out his commodities by little and little, the jester still playing his part, and the musitians singing and playing upon their instruments. The principall things that they sell are oyles, soveraigne waters, amorous songs printed, Apothecary drugs, and a Commonweale of other trifles. The head Mountebanke at every time that he delivereth out any thing, maketh an extemporall speech, which he doth eftsoones intermingle with such savory jests (but spiced now and then with singular scurrility) that they minister passing mirth and laughter to the whole company, which perhaps may consist of a thousand people that flocke together about one of their stages.

Wives and Courtesans

As for the number of these Venetian Cortezans it is very great. . . .

A most ungodly thing without doubt that there should be a tolleration of such licentious wantons in so glorious, so potent, so renowned a city. . . .

For they thinke that the chastity of their wives would be the sooner assaulted, and so consequently they should be capricornified, (which of all the indignities in the world the Venetian cannot patiently endure) were it not for these places of evacuation. But I marvaile how that should be true though these Cortezans were utterly rooted out of the City. For the Gentlemen do even coope up their wives alwaies within the walles of their houses for feare of these inconveniences, as much as if there were no Cortezans at all in the City. So that you shall very seldome see a Venetian Gentleman's wife but either at the solemnization of a great marriage, or at the Christning of a Jew, or late in the evening rowing in a Gondola. . . .

For so infinite are the allurements of these amorous Calypsoes, that the fame of them hath drawen many to Venice from some of the remotest parts of Christendome, to contemplate their beauties, and enjoy their pleasing dalliances. And indeede such is the variety of the delicious objects they minister to their lovers, that they want nothing tending to delight. For when you come into one of their Palaces (as indeed some few of the principallest of them live in very magnificent and portly buildings fit for the entertainement of a great Prince) you seeme to enter into the Paradise of Venus. For their fairest roomes are most glorious and glittering to behold. . . .

As for her selfe shee comes to thee decked like the Queene and Goddesse of love, in so much that thou wilt thinke she made a late transmigration from Paphos, Cnidos, or Cythera, the auncient habitations of Dame Venus. For her face is adorned with the quintessence of beauty. In her cheekes thou shalt see the Lilly and the Rose strive for the supremacy, and the silver tramels of her haire displayed in that curious manner besides her two frisled peakes standing up like pretty Pyramides, that they give thee the true Cos amoris.

The Game of Balloo

Here every Sunday and Holy-day in the evening the young men of the citie doe exercise themsalves at a certaine play that they call Baloone, which is thus: Sixe or seven yong men or thereabout weare certaine round things upon their armes, made of timber, which are full of sharpe pointed knobs cut out of the same matter. In these exercises they put off their doublets, and having put this round instrument upon one of their armes, they tosse up and downe a great ball, as great as our football in England: sometimes they will tosse the ball with this instrument, as high as a common Church, and about one hundred paces at the least from them.

The Strappado

On the fourth day of August being Thursday, I saw a very Tragicall and dolefull spectacle in Saint Markes place. Two men tormented with the strapado, which is done in this manner. The offender having his hands bound behind him, is conveighed into a rope that hangeth in a pully, and after hoysed up in the rope to a great heigth with two severall swinges, where he sustaineth so great torments that his joynts are for the time loosed and pulled asunder; besides such abundance of bloud is gathered into his hands and face, that for the time he is in the torture, his face and hands doe looke as red as fire.

Tortoises and Gentlemen in the Market

Amongst many other strange fishes that I have observed in their market places, I have seene many Torteises, whereof I never saw but one in all England. Besides they have great plenty of fowle, and such admirable variety thereof, that I have heard in the citie they are furnished with no lesse then two hundred severall sortes of them. I have observed a thing amongst the Venetians, that I have not a little wondred at, that their Gentlemen and greatest Senators, a man worth perhaps two millions of duckats, will come into the market, and buy their flesh, fish, fruites, and such other things as are necessary for the maintenance of their family: a token indeed of frugality, which is commendable in all men; but me thinkes it is not an argument of true generosity, that a noble spirit should deject it selfe to these petty and base matters, that are fitter to be done by servants then men of a generose parentage. Therefore I commend mine owne countrey-man, the English Gentleman, that scorneth to goe into the market to buy his victuals and other necessaries for house-keeping, but employeth his Cooke or Cator about those inferior and sordid affaires.

The Robes of Gentlemen

It is said there are of all the Gentlemen of Venice, which are there called Clarissimoes, no lesse then three thousand, all which when they goe abroad out of their houses, both they that beare office, and they that are private, doe weare gownes: wherein they imitate Romanos rerum Dominos, gentemque togatam. Most of their gownes are made of blacke cloth, and over their left shoulder they have a flappe made of the same cloth, and edged with blacke Taffata: Also most of their gownes are faced before with blacke

Taffata: There are others also that weare other gownes according to their distinct offices and degrees; as they that are of the Councell of tenne (which are as it were the maine body of the whole estate) doe most commonly weare blacke chamlet gownes, with marveilous long sleeves, that reach almost downe to the ground. Againe they that weare red chamlet gownes with long sleeves, are those that are called Savi, whereof some have authority onely by land, as being the principall Overseers of the Podesta'es and Prætors in their land cities, and some by Sea. There are others also that weare blew cloth gownes with blew flapps over their shoulders, edged with Taffata. These are the Secretaries of the Councell of tenne. Upon every great festivall day the Senators, and greatest Gentlemen that accompany the Duke to Church, or to any other place, doe weare crimson damaske gownes, with flappes of crimson velvet cast over their left shoulders. Likewise the Venetian Knights weare blacke damaske gownes with long sleeves: but hereby they are distinguished from the other Gentlemen. For they weare red apparell under their gownes, red silke stockings, and red pantafles. All these gowned men doe weare marveilous little blacke flat caps of felt, without any brimmes at all, and very diminutive falling bandes, no ruffes at all, which are so shallow, that I have seene many of them not above a little inch deepe. The colour that they most affect and use for their other apparel, I mean doublet, hose, and jerkin, is blacke: a colour of gravity and decency.

POSSESSION AND IMPOSTURE

The extracts that follow are from Herford and Simpson, *Ben Jonson's Works*, Vol. IX (1950), pp. 731–2. They relate to Act V, Scene xii, lines 22–35.

25. *vomits crooked pinnes.* In *A Tryal of Witches at the Assizes Held at Bury St. Edmonds . . . on the Tenth day of March, 1664. Before Sir Matthew Hale Kt*, 1682, p. 21, Samuel Pacy, a merchant of Lowestoft, deposed about his two children, supposed to be bewitched: 'At other times They would fall into Swounings, & upon the recovery to their speech they would Cough extreamly, & bring up much Flegme, and with the same crooked Pins, and one time a Two-penny Nail with a very broad head, which Pins (amounting to Forty or more) together with the Two-penny Nail were produced in Court, with the affirmation of the said Deponent, that he was present when the Said Nail was Vomited up, and also most of the Pins.'

27. *His mouth's running away*. Cf. Darrell, *A true Narration of the strange and grevous Vexation by the Devil, of . . . William Somers of Nottingham*, 1600, p. 19: 'He was also continually torne in very fearful manner and disfigured in his face: wherein somtimes his lips were drawne awry, now to the one syde now to the other: somtimes his face and neck distorted, to the right and to the left hand, yea somtimes writhen to his back.'

28, 29. *in his belly . . . in his throate*. Samuel Harsnet, *A Discovery of the fraudulent practises of Iohn Darrel*, 1599, p. 213, quotes Somers's confession of his imposture: 'I did moue first the calfe of my legge, then my knee-bone, which motion of the knee will likewise make a motion or rising of the thigh. Also by drawing and stopping of my wind, my bellie would stirre and shewe a kind of swelling. The bunch (as p. 214 they tearmed it) about my chest, was by the thrusting out of my breast. Likewise my secret swallowing did make the ende of my windepipe to moue, and to shew greater then vsually it is: Againe, by mouing of my iawes, one bunch was easily made in the side, my cheeke neere mine eare: and about the middle of my cheeke with the ende of my tongue thrust against it. These motions by practise I woulde make very fast, one after another: so that there might easily seeme to bee running in my bodie of some thing, from place to place.'

31. *blew toad*. Ibid., p. 53, 'The booke of the boye of Burton' (Thomas Darling, another of Darrell's tools) 'sayeth, that towards the end of the fast for his pretended dispossession, *he began to heaue & lift vehementlie at his stomacke, and getting up some fleagme and choler said (pointing with his finger, and following with his eyes) looke, looke, see you not the mouse that is gone out of my mouth? and so pointed after it, vnto the farthest part of the parlor.*'

APPENDIX II

A SELECTION OF VARIANTS

A. VERBAL VARIANTS (affecting the choice of a word in a modernised text)

The Folio reading has been adopted except where otherwise stated.

The Epistle (see also note on p. 9, line 143)

58	F Yet, to (Q or to)
59	F ingennuously (Q ingeniously)
77	F severe (Q grave)
82	F among (Q in)
88	F filth (Q garbage)

The Prologue

1	F yet (Q God)

Act I

1.1.34	F shares, I fat [one copy] (Q F [*corrected*] shares; fat) [Q adopted]
1.2.70	F Selves (Q Themselves)
1.2.75	F Eene his (Q His very)
1.2.82	F adds in margin *One knocks/without.*
1.2.88	F Without (Q Within)
1.2.100	F without (Q within)
1.3.66	F adds in margin *Another knocks.*
1.4.28	F I doe conceive you (Q I conceive you)
1.4.60	F What then did (Q But what did)
1.4.159	F adds in margin *Another knocks.*
1.5.37	F adds in margin *They embrace.*
1.5.84	F adds in margin *Another knocks.*

Act II

2.1.50	F *Arch-dukes!* (Q Arch-duke,)
2.1.64	F knew (Q know)
2.2.67	F 't makes (Q makes)
2.2.81–2	F or of thee (Q or the)
2.2.109	F adds in margin *Pointing to his/bill and his/glasse.*
2.2.153	F besides (Q beside)

2.2.222 F adds in margin CELIA *at the/windo' throwes/downe her/handkerchiefe.*
2.3.1 F Spight o' (Q Bloud of)
2.3.2 F adds in margin *He beates away/the montebanke/&c.*
2.3.16 F lose (Q loose)
2.4.6 F [*corrected*] an (Q F [*uncorrected*] some)
2.5.66 F adds in margin *Knocke within.*
2.6.75 F who (Q that)

Act III

3.2.60 F It is (Q Is is)
3.3.20 F adds in margin *One knocks.*
3.4.90 F MONTAGNIE (Q Montagnié) [Q adopted]
3.6.2 F adds in margin *One knockes.*
3.7.10 F adds in margin *To Bonario.*
3.7.119 F thy thy (Q thy) [Q adopted]
3.7.139 F adds in margin *He leapes off/from his couch.*
3.7.172 F lose (Q loose)
3.7.266 F adds in margin *He leapes out/from where/Mosca had/plac'd him.*
3.8.15 F adds in margin *They knock/without.*

Act IV

4.1.15 F with (Q with with)
4.1.57 F too (Q two)
4.4.15 F adds in margin *To Voltore.*
4.4.16 F doth (Q do's)
4.4.17 F adds in margin *To Corbaccio.*
4.4.20 F adds in margin *To Corvino, then/to Voltore a-/gaine.*
4.5.4 F So, the yong man (Q So has the youth)
4.5.43 F goodnesse (Q vertue)
4.5.72 F lords (Q *Sires*)
4.5.127 F shame (Q harme)
4.5.130 F catholique (Q *Christian*)
4.5.132 F adds in margin *She swownes.*
4.6.20 F adds in margin *Volpone is/brought in, as/impotent.*

Act V

5.1.12 F adds in margin *He drinkes.*
5.1.16 F adds in margin *Drinkes againe.*
5.2.102 F adds in margin *Cestus.* [Q adopted]

5.3.8	F adds in margin *Volpone peepes/from behinde a/ traverse.*
5.3.114	F *Commandatori* (Q *Commandadori*)
5.4.47	F adds in margin *They knocke/without.*
5.4.55	F Fitted (Q Apted)
5.4.61	F adds in margin *They rush in.*
5.4.72	F adds in margin *They pul of the/shel and disco-/ver him.*
5.5.Head	F adds in margin *The first, in the habit of a Com-/ mandadore:/the other, of a/Clarissimo.*
5.8.24	F adds in margin *Mosca walkes/by 'hem.*
5.10.30	F some-deale (Q somewhere)
5.10.50	F it cannot be, but he is possest, grave fathers. (Q It cannot be (my *Sires*) but he is possest).
5.12.15	F adds in margin *Volpone whis-/pers the Advo-/cate.*
5.12.23	F adds in margin *Voltore falls.*
5.12.54	F o' the hinge (Q on the henge)
5.12.84	F adds in margin *He puts off his/disguise.*
5.12.130	F thy state (Q thy'estate)

B. PUNCTUATION VARIANTS

Although a slight prejudice in favour of the Quarto punctuation is suggested by the textual hypothesis outlined on page xxxii, there are a number of instances in which the Folio departures from the Quarto are apparently deliberate. They have been taken by Herford and Simpson as evidence of authorial revision, and by de Vocht as proof of the Folio editor's limited competence. Many are likely, however, to be the work of compositors intervening to conform the text to printing-house convention. None are of great importance, but some affect the pace, inflexion or significance of certain passages.

In a number of instances the Folio replaces Quarto dashes with full stops. In the present text the Quarto dashes have been retained at 3.7.111 (ask—), 3.7.122 (satisfy—), 5.10.26 (fathers—), 5.12.103 (fathers—), 5.12.145 (judgements—). In all these cases the sense appears to gain by being represented as incomplete. Where the thought appears complete, however, the Quarto dashes have been dropped (as in the Folio): e.g. at 5.10.19 (Q all—), and at 5.12.59 (Q gentleman—).

The Quarto often uses colons, semi-colons or even commas at the end of speeches, and the Folio substitutes a full stop. This edition follows the Folio where it appears to observe the modern practice of using a stop when a thought is complete—the stops ought not to be allowed to lessen the pace of the dialogue; it treats the Quarto punctuation as a suspension mark where the thought appears incomplete. Thus the Folio has been followed at (e.g.) 1.2.111 (Q Mosca;), 1.5.67 (Q means;), and 2.2.38 (Q Piazza;). But the Quarto has been interpreted by a dash at 3.7.72 (Q you,), 3.7.124 (Q ruin:), 4.6.16 (Q consciences:), 4.6.73 (Q fault:), 4.6.80 (Q it,), 5.2.98 (Q oils,).

Two longer speeches affected by conspicuous differences of scoring between Quarto and Folio are 3.7.240–60 and 2.2.133–70. In both cases I have preferred the Folio. In Celia's long speech (3.7.240–60) the Quarto offers eight dashes in six lines (pierc'd—, open'd—, touch'd—, you—, *Saints*—, *Heaven*—, scape—), and has been held to make the speech more vehement and impulsive; the Folio reaches a climax, however, with much better control.

KING ALFRED'S COLLEGE
LIBRARY

Printed in Great Britain by
The Garden City Press Limited, Letchworth, Hertfordshire